BAND BETTERMENT

EDWIN FRANKO GOLDMAN

BAND BETTERMENT

Suggestions and Advice to Bands,
Bandmasters, and Band-players

By

EDWIN FRANKO GOLDMAN
Mus. Doc.

1934

Published by

CARL FISCHER, Inc.

62 Cooper Square

NEW YORK, U. S. A.

BOSTON

CHICAGO

DEDICATED

to

the cause of Bands and Band Music

Copyright 1934
by CARL FISCHER, Inc.
New York

PRINTED IN U. S. A.
MAJOR PRESS, INC.

CONTENTS

FOREWORD V

EDWIN FRANKO GOLDMAN VI

CHAPTER   PART I   PAGE

1. The Mission of Music 1

2. Music as an Avocation 6

3. Which Instrument Shall I Choose? 11

4. When to Begin 14

5. The Personal Relation Between Teacher and Pupil 17

6. Wind Instrument Playing from a Hygienic Viewpoint 20

7. The Benefits of Ensemble Playing 22

                         PART II

8. Instruments of the Band 24

9. Comparison of the Band and Orchestra 36

10. The Conductor 44

11. Rehearsals 50

12. Programs 55

13. The Library 60

14. Seating Arrangement 66

15. Intonation 71

16. Sight Reading 74

17. Pointers in Phrasing 78

18. Slow or Sustained Movements 82

19. The Playing of Marches 86

20. Outdoor Music 96

21. Band Contests 101

22. Massed Bands 105

23. Band Camps 109

CONTENTS

PART III

CHAPTER   PAGE

24. Saxophones 111

25. The Cornet and Trumpet 115

26. The Cornet Soloist 120

27. Other Solo Instruments 124

28. Suitable Solos and how to Play Them 126

29. Cadenzas . . . . . °. 131

PART IV

30. How to Improve Bands 134

31. Pointers for Bandsmen 139

32. Important Suggestions for Wind Instrument Players 145

33. The Playing of Two Instruments 150

34. Nervousness and How to Overcome It 154

35. The Care of Brass Instruments 157

36. The Care of Reed Instruments 160

37. Criticism 161

38. Envy Among Musicians 165

39. The Real Fakir and the Real Artist 168

40. Amateur vs. Professional 171

41. A Great Future Need 174

42. The Band from an educational, artistic and cultural viewpoint. Opinions of famous orchestral conductors, composers, and other famous men 176

ILLUSTRATIONS

                                         PAGE

Edwin Franko Goldman . . . . Frontispiece

John Philip Sousa and Edwin Franko Goldman 35

The Goldman Band 65

A Goldman Band Concert on the Mall 95

Ottorino Respighi and Edwin Franko Goldman 114

Charter Members of the American Bandmasters' Association 170

FOREWORD

This work is not intended as a technical treatise in any sense of the word, for there are many worthwhile books on all important band subjects. This volume is the result of my studies and my observations. Having been identified with bands since my childhood I have learned to know their needs and their weaknesses. If this book helps in any way to raise the standard of bands and band music, if it proves of any service to bandmasters, I shall feel well repaid for my efforts.

EDWIN FRANKO GOLDMAN.

EDWIN FRANKO GOLDMAN

In his choice of a career, Edwin Franko Goldman had little difficulty. As the child of a family of musicians, he was predestined to be a musician himself. His mother was Selma Franko, one of the famous Franko family who in the late sixties of the past century, toured Europe and America as child prodigies. She played both violin and piano and made a number of appearances with Adelina Patti. His father was a lawyer and a talented amateur violinist and musical scholar. His uncles were the famous Nahan Franko, celebrated violinist and conductor at the Metropolitan Opera House and Sam Franko, noted violinist, teacher and musicologist. Other musical connections in his family include the Hollaenders, Gustave, director of the famous Stern Conservatory in Berlin, and Victor, well known as a composer.

Mr. Goldman was born in Louisville, Kentucky, but at the age of eight came with his parents to New York, after brief periods of residence in Terre Haute and Evansville, Indiana. Like many a boy, he wanted to play the cornet . . . and he did. He early convinced his teachers, George Wiegand, Carl Sohst and others, of his immense talent for the instrument, and at the age of fourteen was given a scholarship by the National Conservatory. A year later, the renowned master, Jules Levy, accepted him as a free pupil. His ten-year association with the Metropolitan Opera Orchestra began when he was a lad of seventeen and already a famous cornetist. Before he was thirty he had played in orchestras and bands under most of the great conductors of the day: Gustave Mahler, Camille Saint-Saens, Luigi Mancinelli, Anton Dvorak, Alfred Hertz, Walter Damrosch, Emil Paur, Felix Mottl, Engelbert Humperdinck, Arturo Toscanini, and his own uncles Nahan and Sam Franko, among others. During this time Mr. Goldman also made a name for himself as cornet soloist, and as organizer and conductor of small ensembles which were in great demand.

For thirteen years Mr. Goldman devoted his entire energies

to teaching the Cornet and Trumpet. Pupils came to him from all over the United States and from many foreign lands as well. On the basis of his experience as a teacher, he has written numerous aids to' the study of these instruments. Probably no other musician of his calibre is as well qualified to write of the Cornet and Trumpet. Mr. Goldman is also known as the composer of many works for various brass instruments, and particularly of many cornet solos which have everywhere found favor.

In 1918, Mr. Goldman gave up teaching in order to give his efforts to the formation of the band which bears his name. To do this, he had to be organizer, director and impressario all in one. His idea was to give free band concerts which might be enjoyed by all. To do this financial backing was necessary, a location had to be found, the finest musicians in New York had to be secured. All this he did after he had been told repeatedly that it was impossible. But Mr. Goldman had faith in his great idea: a new and greater type of band, and the success of his enterprise was greater than even he had dared to hope.

Today the Goldman Band has been pronounced by all critics to be unique and to have no superior in the world. Its annual summer concerts and frequent appearances on the radio have been heard by millions. Mr. Goldman's efforts toward raising the standards of bands and band-music have earned him the reputation of being the creator of the modern symphony band. In the interests of bands, Mr. Goldman has traveled many times to all parts of the United States in order to advise and inspire others, giving generously and altruistically of his time. In appreciation of his endeavors Mr. Goldman has been honored by presentations from dozens of universities, bands and other organizations, and has been the recipient of many official honors. He is the first musician ever officially to be honored by the City of New York. Boston and many other cities have presented him with their "keys." The Commonwealth of Massachusetts has presented him with a gold pin bearing the official seal. His fame has traveled even across the ocean, for in 1929 the French Government through its Consul in New York, made him an "Officier de l'Instruction Publique." In 1933, the decoration and rank of Cavaliere of the Order of the Crown of Italy was conferred upon Mr. Goldman by the Royal Italian Consul in New York on behalf of King Victor Emmanuel III. In April, 1934, an honorary degree, that of

Doctor of Music, was conferred upon Mr. Goldman by Phillips University. Mr. Goldman is also Founder and Honorary Life President of the American Bandmasters' Association.

The Goldman Band has been identified with radio since the very start of broadcasting and has always been one of the most popular and pleasing organizations on the air. It is said that more people have heard this band than any other organization in the world. The visible audiences at the concerts on the Mall in Central Park and on the Campus at New York University are estimated at from fifteen thousand to thirty thousand people nightly. It is claimed that Mr. Goldman is known by sight to more people than any other person in New York.

Mr. Goldman's marches are too well known to need naming. No one can seriously contest his right to be known as the successor to John Philip Sousa. The first time the two famous bandmasters met, Sousa said, "I've always wanted to tell you that I am greatly indebted to your mother's family for much of my success." Goldman was taken aback momentarily, but recovered quickly enough to allow Sousa to continue with his explanation.

"The first time that I heard really fine music was when the Franko family of five wonderfully talented children came to Washington for a concert. It was the first time I had heard real music and it inspired me with a zeal to do better." Sousa in his autobiography entitled "Marching Along" wrote those very words in one of the first chapters of the book.

Goldman paused for a few seconds after listening to the story told by his new friend, and then replied, "Mr. Sousa, you may be interested to know that you yourself have been a great source of inspiration to me."

And both agreed that life had a most unusual way of its own. Here was the great Sousa inspired as a boy by the famous Franko children: uncles, aunts and mother of Edwin Franko Goldman. Sousa later became the world's most famous bandmaster. Goldman inherited the musical tradition of his family, and as a boy became inspired by Sousa. In later years the two bandmasters met and became close friends. A strange coincidence indeed!

The death of Sousa in March 1932, left a great void in Goldman's life. Since the passing of Sousa, Goldman has paid his close friend many tributes. In August, 1932, the famous Goldman Band in the midst of its fifteenth season on the Mall in Central Park devoted its fiftieth concert to Sousa, and during the program Mrs. Sousa presented Mr. Goldman with the baton her husband used in conducting, saying she knew that would have been his wish. Mr. Goldman wrote a special march for this occasion and named it "Tribute to Sousa."

In presenting Mr. Goldman's book on bands, based on his unusual experience, the Publishers feel certain that it will prove a most welcome, helpful and authoritative addition to the none too large literature on the subject.

THE PUBLISHERS.

PART I.

CHAPTER I

THE MISSION OF MUSIC

In the unconscious enjoyment of music, how many people realize to what dim and far-distant ages its memories hark back? Long before civilization, with the crudest of "noise makers", our savage forbears produced and loved their music. It was associated with their tribal festivities, with their religious rites, with all the invocations and incantations to their various deities. Music was the power which swayed their gods, and music was a stimulant to their zeal and fervor. It drove out their evil spirits, and propitiated the benign spirits, and in very truth, soothed the "savage breast".

All through the rise and forward march of civilization, we find music playing an important part in the daily life of peoples all over the world. Soldiers marched to war to the inspiring strains of music; they were urged on to the heat of battle by their heroic bands; and welcomed home again with happy song and joyous melody. Today we put music to even more varied uses than ever before in history. Great medical authorities agree as to its power to help the sick and ailing. Criminologists testify to its softening influence upon the unfortunate ones who have strayed from the paths of law and order, and within four walls are paying their penalties. Even the hopelessly insane are calmed and made happier by hearing music. Old people, tired with the struggles of life, renew their youth and review their achievements while listening to lovely music; young people are inspired to greater effort and better things through the stimulus of music. We have music in the parks, where the city's poor and less favored children may listen and learn, and in listening, forget for a while the difficulties and burdens of the daily battle of life. We have music in the schools, good music, and much music; let it be a part of the lives of our little ones, that the love for it may be bred in them from babyhood. We

---

Simplicity, truth and naturalness are the great principles of the beautiful in all productions of art.—*Beethoven.*

I

have music in all our public institutions, and all unite to praise its wonderfully helpful qualities wherever its appeal is heard.

Certainly the ennobling and broadening qualities of music cannot be gainsaid, since all peoples, all sects, all religions are united in music. Where is the man or woman who does not respond to the wonderful appeal of the organ in church, or who does not feel better after listening for a while to sweet and harmonious sounds, whether they be the music of voice or instrument?

And is it not eminently fitting and proper, inasmuch as music is harmony, that it should be the method and means of bringing harmony into the lives of people; that it should help to make men realize that they are brethren, and that there can be no real brotherhood without harmony? An orchestra or a body of singers does not divide itself into two parts for the purpose of playing or singing two melodies entirely opposed one to the other, and each trying to outstrip the other. No beauty, harmony or pleasure could accrue from such an arrangement, or rather, disarrangement. No, "the house divided against itself must fall," whether it be a musical house, or the "house of nations" or the "house of man". But, in the orchestra, all playing together under one leader, each awaiting his cue and giving each co-player his chance and uniting in one great effort for perfect coordination that gives the great, the beautiful and the perfect result which is music, melody and harmony. And in the Brotherhood of Man, each one bearing and forbearing with his neighbor, giving, in the spirit of greatest love, taking, in the spirit of graciousness and gratitude, giving each his chance and joining one and all, great and small, for a common betterment, a greater good—this in truth were harmony, the greatest, the sweetest and deepest harmony. If music, in this analogy, brings any response to its mission; if through its appeal to man's higher thought and better nature it can help to bring men's lives into more perfect accord; if the absolute harmony of music can be translated into the harmony of right thought and right living, then indeed is the mission of music divinely ordained and divinely sent. Then indeed is the connection established between music and the tribal rites of savages; music and the brethren temporarily astray; music and the organ in church; music and the Brotherhood of Man, where one leadership is followed, one voice is heard, and the result, harmony!

Music is the child of prayer, the companion of religion.—*Chateaubriand*.

Of all the arts, music is indeed the most sociological, exerting a greater influence over people than any or all of the other arts. Music has always been called the universal language. It makes no difference from what country or clime one comes, music is the one language that is intelligible to all. Only the deaf are deprived of its benefits and blessings. It has been said that the deaf are generally sadder than the blind. This is because the sense of hearing is so much more necessary than that of sight, to the perception of life about us.

Then again, it is not only between men that music has its mission, but also between men and animals—and even between animals themselves.

Music establishes mutualities, which though they be quite vague, it alone of all the arts is able to create. The animal does not recognize language itself—but only the musical elements of language—such as the intonation, quantity or quality or the intensity of sound. It is the intonation which we employ, either affectionate or severe, which draws it to us or rebuffs it. It heeds the voice and not the speech. Even the brute beasts are attracted to and affected by musical instruments. The old saying "Music hath charms to soothe the savage breast" is true indeed. We have all heard how the serpent listens to, and perhaps understands, the sweet tones of the flute.

Coming back to what was said before, music is the one art which all peoples can understand, and it is this fact which makes it the most important of all the arts. All the arts are wonderful, but none of them leaves the lasting impression that music does— nor do they have as great an influence for good. Music is for the people. One does not require a college education to enjoy it. In fact, one requires no education at all. There is scarcely a person alive who does not love music in some form or other. We often hear of people who do not care for classical music— or as they call it, "high-brow" music. We all love the things with which we are familiar. We love the tunes which we learned in our childhood, we love the songs of our country, we love the religious tunes we have learned to know through the church and synagogue. Those who are fortunate enough to hear the music of the masters frequently enough to become familiar with it, derive untold pleasure and satisfaction from it. If, for instance, we were to hear Beethoven's Eroica Symphony, Haydn's

---

Music can move or melt an audience, and ought therefore to be made a powerful auxiliary to the faithful preacher.—*Lowell Mason.*

Military Symphony, or Wagner's Love Death from Tristan and Isolde, we would love and cherish them as we do the simple tunes we learned in our childhood, or some of the popular tunes which are drummed into our ears day in and out for months at a time. The so-called popular songs of the day outlive their usefulness in a few months and die. Really fine music lives forever. We cannot hear the music of the masters too often. Bach, Mozart and Beethoven lived generations ago, but their music is still played in all corners of the earth, and as the years go on this music is played more and more. Its mission never will end. It brings joy and solace, and the oftener we hear it the more we love it. We hear new beauties in it at each performance.

To prove my assertion that music has the greatest influence of all the arts, I need only say that people come together in greater and more enthusiastic numbers at the call of music, than to gaze at pictures or statuary or architectural beauties. Music in its very demand for silence stifles every discordant and alien voice. To those who are in doubt as to how wonderfully this effect is achieved, it should be suggested that they attend a large gathering where only the best music is performed by a symphony orchestra or a band. Speaking from my own experience, I do not know of a more inspiring sight than can be seen at our concerts. Audiences of from fifteen to thirty thousand and more nightly sit as though spell-bound throughout the music. Not a move, not a sound. Rich, poor, educated, illiterate, people of all classes and types, people from all countries, the most cosmopolitan assemblage in the world, drawn together by music, the language of the universe. They all understand it. They know and feel whether it is solemn, joyous, humorous or heroic. It touches their hearts, sends them to their homes with renewed interest in life, has made them forget themselves and their worries. Music is the people's art. The rich can purchase the best and most expensive instruments, but with very few exceptions the greatest composers and performers have come from the people—the very poor people. It is the exception for a musical genius to come from the rich. But it is in many instances through the rich that the people at large are given the opportunity of hearing good music. Most of our symphony orchestras, chamber music organizations, opera com-

---

It is time that is at once the most necessary, the most difficult, and the most essential requisite in music.—*Mozart*.

panies, etc., are maintained through the generosity of public spirited citizens. It is true, that many of our concerts are still too high-priced for the poor to take advantage of them, but here in America—and particularly in New York—more is being done each year to bring good music within the reach of all.

To invent beautiful forms of rhythm is a thing that cannot be taught. It is one of the rarest gifts in music; rhythm itself is, moreover, the least developed part of modern music.—*Berlioz*.

CHAPTER II

MUSIC AS AN AVOCATION

THE PART IT PLAYS IN OUR LIVES

There is no denying the fact that music is the most democratic,—the most popular, and the greatest of all the arts, for it is the one art that can be made intelligible to all peoples, no matter from what country cr clime they may come. In our own country today music is being cultivated more seriously and more extensively than ever before.

The question is frequently asked now, "Is it worthwhile training to become a professional musician?" This question has been asked me so many times during the past few years, that I have given it considerable thought. The change in musical conditions due to the advent of the radio, filmed music, phonograph music, and such purely mechanical triumphs has given us food for thought.

It is true that thousands of musicians have been ousted from their positions during the past few years, for various reasons. Orchestras have been eliminated in most of the Movie Theatres, because of the fact that the music and the pictures are recorded and produced from the same film whereas formerly large orchestras were featured and music was a great factor. This, unfortunately, is only so in a very few instances, today. In former years every theatre had an orchestra, even though the production was a comedy or drama requiring no music. This orchestra played an overture as well as numbers between the acts. Today only those plays calling for music in the production have orchestras.

Years ago every hotel of importance employed a small orchestra to play during luncheon and dinner, and frequently for purely concert or dance purposes, and some of these orchestras were of fair size and excellent quality. One of the great attractions of the old Waldorf-Astoria in New York, and the Plaza

---

Many a man of genius perishes because he has to gain his bread by teaching, instead of devoting himself to study.—*Haydn.*

Hotel were their daily concerts by fine orchestras. Such orchestras have become practically obsolete. Even some of the Dance Halls today secure their music from the Radio or the Phonograph. Many of our Symphony Orchestras, Bands and other musical organizations have had to disband because of lack of support. In fact, all of our Symphony Orchestras and Opera Companies are suffering.

What, then, is the future of music and musicians? In the future there will be only room for the very best performers. The demands made upon players today is so very great, that only the very best will be able to survive. We are undergoing a great change. We are living in a new age. Musical conditions will adjust themselves just as business conditions will. This may take considerable time, but a new era is dawning, and we will have to accustom ourselves to the new conditions. Many orchestral musicians of the past will have to seek livelihood in other ways unless they can take up the profession of teaching, which at present seems overcrowded. It is a sad state of affairs for those who have spent many years of their lives at music and who are not fitted for any other type of work, but there are, and have been for the last few years, too many professional musicians. It must be remembered that players come to America from every country on the globe. They were received here with open arms, until now, when there is no work for them. In no other country in the world would they have been permitted to enter as they have here. It is too bad that some kind of limit was not put on the "musical" immigration some years ago. Of course, we needed foreign musicians, and we want them yet, if they are *better* than those we have—but we certainly did not need all those who came over. I firmly believe in having the very best for our Symphony Orchestras and Bands, regardless of nationality, but if the American is on a par with the foreigner, I believe he deserves the preference.

There *is* and *will be* a future in music for those who are possessed of unusual talent and ability. These of course, are not in the majority. All professions are overcrowded—but there is always an opportunity for the really capable ones, those of great talent—those who have a real message to convey. Under such circumstances, why should anyone of mediocre ability or capacity want to enter the musical profession? Naturally, many are misguided by the praise of admiring friends or incapable

---

Were it not for music, we might in these days say, the Beautiful is dead.—*D'Israeli.*

or unscrupulous teachers. Many enter the profession firmly believing themselves to be possessed of great talent, and after years of struggle they find out that they cannot make the desired grade. It is a serious proposition with which one is confronted in making a decision for a career, and one which must be weighed from many angles and with great care. The serious student of music studies and works for years to prepare and perfect himself, and after he has reached a certain degree of proficiency he has to study constantly and diligently every day of his life to maintain and improve his technique and his art. New artists are developed constantly so that one has always to keep on the alert.

As mentioned before, there will always be opportunities in music, but, only those of great talent should be encouraged to take up music as a profession. I believe, however, that every child should be given the opportunity of learning to play some instrument—not with the idea of becoming a professional musician, for that would be a calamity indeed—but rather as an avocation. The child who acquires an early interest in music will have an avocation, a hobby, as long as he lives. Affording an opportunity to learn to play an instrument is one of the most valuable gifts parents can give to their children. The child who plays an instrument is not the one who loiters about the street corners idling away his time and getting into mischief, for he has something to occupy his spare time. He can pass many pleasant hours playing, practicing new music— playing with others. As long as he lives, this child will have an avocation, for music will become a part of his life. The jails are not filled with those who play musical instruments. The child who learns music and plays an instrument will like all the better things that life offers. He will be interested in all the finer things—painting—sculpture—literature—architecture, etc. Think only of the cultural advantages the study of music offers.

In former days people who wanted music in the home had to create it. Parents had children instructed, one on the Piano, another the Violin, and a third the Cello. In this way they eventually had music in the home, a "family orchestra." Naturally parents did not always select the proper instruments for their children. It often happens that one who is taught the

---

Music is not a mere pastime. Its effects are both powerful and beneficial, not only upon the cultured few, but upon the uncultured many.—*Haweis.*

Violin and does not progress satisfactorily, may be successful with the Piano if given the opportunity. No child should be deprived of the opportunity of learning to play some instrument. People have become somewhat "musically lazy" of late years because of the Radio, Phonograph and other mechanical musical devices. It is so easy to press a button and hear a great variety of music, good, bad, and indifferent—never enough good music. This button can bring during the day, dozens of Jazz Orchestras, crooners, singers, instrumentalists of all descriptions, a Symphony Orchestra, and a fine band occasionally, and even opera performances. Of course, one of the blessings of the Radio is that a person can press that same little button and turn it off. Radio is indeed a great blessing, but as I said before, it has made people "musically lazy". They have grown accustomed to securing their music so easily that they begin to believe it is not worthwhile to have their children take up the study of an instrument. This is a great mistake for if people play, they will certainly appreciate music more, and become more interested. Not everyone would or could become a fine player; but one should always strive for improvement and, after all, *the great joy in music is in being able to make it yourself.*

Music plays an important part in our lives either consciously or unconsciously from the cradle to the grave. The young baby is sung to sleep to the strains of a soothing lullaby. After a very few years he goes to kindergarten and learns the joyful children's songs. Then he goes to school and learns the songs of his country—the patriotic songs. He next goes to church, and becomes familiar with the religious tunes. Later he gets married to the strains of Wagner's Bridal music and Mendelssohn's Wedding March. People are buried to the strains of music, and it is often said they are greeted in heaven with harps —or trumpets—or both.

It is apparent that music does play a very important part all through our lives. We cannot have much enjoyment without music. We cannot dance without it. Under the circumstances we should give it more thought. We should encourage our children in the study of it, and give them something that is lacking in most of their lives now—something that will make better men and women of them. We should give every possible consideration to our worthwhile "living musical organizations" whether they be Orchestras, Bands, Choruses, or other types

---

Such sweet compulsion doth in music lie.—*Milton.*

of ensembles. All artists and organizations need encouragement. They cannot exist without it. They require two kinds
of support, financial and moral. Everyone can give either one
or the other, and many can give both. Only an interested public
can restore some of our organizations and help maintain them.
Radio is a great blessing—so is the phonograph. They have
brought music to places it would never have reached otherwise.
But give a thought to living music.

We want everybody to be a music lover. We want everybody to follow music as a hobby—an avocation. Through this
everybody will be benefitted. The professional will secure the
encouragement and support he requires and the field of his
activities will be broadened. The amateur will secure all the
benefits, all the happiness and all the cultural advantages which
the art of music has to offer. Those who play for the love of
the art—for the pleasure of it—are to be envied for they are
happy indeed.

Music should not be considered a luxury—for it is not.
It is a necessity—a great one—more so in these trying days
than ever before. It is false economy to eliminate music in
our endeavor to curtail expenses, for no matter how much we
have, it is not enough. Music is the key to health and happiness.

To be really impressed by music, we should, as it were, actually feel the vibrations
of the instruments and voices.—*Berlioz*.

CHAPTER III

WHICH INSTRUMENT SHALL I CHOOSE?

"Which wind-instrument should I take up?" is a question which has been asked so frequently of late that a few remarks concerning such choice seem opportune. For the past ten years the study of wind-instruments has become more and more popular, and there is probably a larger number of amateur bands in the country than of orchestras. Thousands who have probably never played any instrument before are now studying a wind-instrument of some kind. The first question that each individual asks when he contemplates taking up an instrument is, "which one shall I play?" There are those, of course, who have a particular fondness for a certain instrument, and in their minds there is no doubt as to which they will choose.

Of course, it is very essential to select an instrument that appeals to one. Without a fondness for the instrument chosen, little progress can be made. Very often the favorite instrument is the one to which the player is least adapted, and this is another idea for serious consideration. It must be remembered that to play the flute, clarinet, oboe, bassoon, or saxophone properly all the fingers are necessary. For the brass instruments only three or four fingers are used—except for the slide trombone,—the slide being manipulated entirely by the hand. From the standpoint of fingering it will thus be clearly seen that the reed and wood instruments are more complicated than the brass. The wood and reed instruments also have a larger compass than the brass, and therefore, passages of greater difficulty can be written for them. The reed player also has more notes to read, and more rapid passages to execute than the brass players. Of the reed instruments, the saxophone is probably the easiest to master. This does not mean that anyone can take it up and in a short time play it satisfactorily. To play any instrument, no matter whether it be the flute, clarinet, cornet or drum, requires

---

Melody alone constitutes the essence of all music.—*J. Raff.*

regular and systematic practice, if good results are to be obtained, and good players are not developed in one, two or three months. It takes considerable time to master any instrument.

The oboe is probably the most difficult of all the reed instruments. Very few amateurs take it up for this reason. Those who take it up professionally are mostly performers who have played some other instrument first. The bassoon, as well, is an instrument which few amateurs take up. The flute has always been a great favorite with amateurs. The clarinet is more of a band and orchestra instrument than a solo instrument, and as such is highly important.

The cornet, alto, baritone, valve trombone, and tuba are all played along the same lines. The method of tone production, as well as the fingering on each is the same. As far as the fingering is concerned, there is nothing easier than one of the brass instruments, but the acquiring of an embouchure is not such an easy matter. The lips must be properly developed through a course of systematic exercises, which must be practiced daily.

Of the brass instruments, the alto is by far the easiest to master, as it requires the least lip development. The alto, however, is not an instrument that is used in many professional bands. The French Horn is another instrument which not enough amateurs take up. It is the most delicate, and at the same time the most difficult of the brass instruments, and great lip development is necessary in order to play it properly. There are excellent opportunities for players of this instrument, as the demand for them is great. The slide trombone is, of course, a popular instrument, but one that is rarely played as it deserves to be. Because of the fact that it has no valves, the player must get his different tones by a movement of the slide, which he pushes back and forth. Unless the player develops his ear he will generally play this instrument badly out of tune.

Drum players, who form an important part of each musical organization, must not be forgotten. The drum section, with all its traps and paraphernalia makes a strong appeal to many people. A really good drummer is an artist just as is the fine performer on any other instrument.

But let us return once more to our original question as to "Which of these instruments shall I take up?". It is natural,

---

The mania of discussing things which they least understand is a very common fault in men.—*Gluck*.

of course that each one wants to take up an instrument that can be used for solo purposes, and that has an interesting part to play in the band or orchestra. Not all the instruments are ideal for parlor use, but each is interesting when taking its part in ensemble music. Each individual instrument is a necessary and important part of a band. We can't all play the cornet or the flute, and not everyone can play the first cornet part. We must have tuba players, and we must have clarinet players. First of all, choose an instrument which you like. If, after trying it for a while, you find you are not adapted to it, change to one of the others with which you may have more success. If your fingers are stiff and clumsy, do not take up one of the reed instruments, which necessitates the use of all of them. If you want to make music your profession, it makes little or no difference upon which instrument you decide, because you are going to study it thoroughly and systematically. Players of all wind instruments should have good teeth, particularly the brass players. Those who wish to take up a brass instrument are often misguided by persons who advise them poorly. A person with thin lips is often advised that he can play the cornet, just as a person with medium-sized or larger lips is often told he cannot play anything but the trombone, baritone or tuba. This kind of advice would seem quite natural and often works out properly, but it must be remembered that the person with thin lips often makes an admirable tuba player, while the one with larger lips frequently develops into a remarkable cornetist. This is just a reminder that it is impossible to tell by one's lips just what instrument he might be best adapted to. As a matter of fact, some with perfectly formed mouths and teeth are often unable to achieve any results on any instrument.

If you are taking up the study of any instrument solely for your own pleasure and recreation, select the one that appeals to you most. If you find that you are not adapted to it, there are plenty of others to choose from. If you take up an instrument simply to become a member of a certain band in which you are interested, select an instrument which will be useful to that band, and one which they may need. It is not the easiest matter in the world to advise people what to take up. The purchase of an instrument does not make one a player —neither does the taking of lessons, without daily practice. The person who has patience, and is willing to go "slow but sure" especially at the start, is the one who succeeds.

CHAPTER IV

WHEN TO BEGIN

A Few Practical Reasons Why Wind Instrument Playing Should Be Started Early In Life

It is well known that genius of any kind usually manifests itself at an early age. We read of the little Mozart, giving his first concerts at the age of six and already composing; of the young Handel, astonishing everyone with his performances on the organ at the tender age of seven. We are told that both Chopin and Liszt played their first concerts at the age of nine; that at fifteen Mendelssohn was considered a mature artist; that Saint-Saens, the great French composer, began his study of the piano at the age of two and a half years; that Paganini, the most remarkable violinist of the nineteenth century, at the age of eight had outgrown the instruction of no less than three famous teachers; that Joachim, the greatest violinist of modern times, began his studies at five, and in two years appeared in public, playing a duet concerto for two violins and orchestra, with his master, and so on, down through many years the names become innumerable—not only of youthful pianists, composers and violinists, but of "infant prodigies" in every field of art and science.

From the consideration of the outcropping of genius, it is not a very far cry to the conscious production and nurture of a talent, or of a "natural bent"—or of a mere desire to achieve an accomplishment for one's own pleasure and amusement. These things, too, are well begun at an early age—the study of a wind instrument no less than any other.

Many players were first attracted to the study of a wind instrument through the boy's inherent love of the military and the martial—the kind of music which made their feet tap unconsciously. Then, too, youth is the time of growth, and impressions received during the formative years between eight

---

Song brings of itself a cheerfulness that wakes the heart to joy.—*Euripides.*

and twelve, are more apt to be retained than those of later years. A boy beginning the study of a wind instrument when he is eight or nine years old will be able to play very nicely in a comparatively short time if he is sincere and constant in his practice. This is quite a consideration when one takes into account the fact that in almost all preparatory schools, high schools and colleges, not to mention military academies, and universities, the band or orchestra takes a prominent part and is a potent factor in the social life of the students, so that if a boy can join the band of his school by virtue of his ability to play well, his place is already established for him.

Another important factor in favor of early study and early acquired proficiency is this: In all high schools, orphan asylums, reform schools, and kindred institutions, bands are organized and kept in constant practice, and a wide field is thus offered for competent and intelligent musicians as teachers of these bands, for they nearly all employ instructors of ability and training. This, of course, applies to students who desire to turn their studies to practical use. And finally, if a child is interested in a study he will do well in it, and conversely, if he succeeds in any study he is sure to be interested in it. Every child ought to take up the study of some musical instrument, not alone as an accomplishment, but to develop his sense of music, and rhythm in particular, and his artist-comprehension of what is good and beautiful in general. Anyone who has a hobby has a safety valve, it is said. If a boy has been taught to play correctly from an early age, his interest will continue to grow, and his success will stimulate him to further effort. What better hobby can a boy have to tide him over the dangerous years, when the "street corner gang" and their often too attractive occupations tempt so strongly? A boy trained to good and beautiful things will turn to them naturally when things insidious and evil threaten him on all sides. His wind instrument, above all things, will provide him with all that his imagination needs, for on it, from his earliest practice, he can sound the stirring music of the soldiery, the inspiring hymns of all the nations, and the soft, sweet songs that soothe and appeal. And the physical benefit derived from the study of a wind instrument must not be overlooked. Many a frail boy has developed into a deep-chested, sturdy youth, through the correct breathing

---

The one and only form of music is melody; no music is conceivable without melody, and both are absolutely inseparabl e.—*Richard Wagner.*

and breath control learned in the playing of a wind instrument.

Thus, the advantage of early studying of any musical instrument is three-fold—mental development, physical growth, and social advancement.

Passion, whether great or not, must never be expressed in an exaggerated manner; and music—even in the most harrowing moment—ought never to offend the ear, but should always remain music, which desires to give pleasure.—*Mozart*.

CHAPTER V

THE PERSONAL RELATION BETWEEN TEACHER AND PUPIL

In olden days men came from far and near "to sit at the feet" of some great sage and teacher. Those were the days when, though book learning was little known, people looked up to, and reverenced, men of wisdom and learning. They were the great men of their time and place, and many of them eventually became great men of all times and all places. They encouraged the young to study and to learn, and placed the art of teaching on the highest plane it has ever attained.

And so today, "teacher" should be a name to be spoken with understanding and respect, for in almost every branch of teaching, years must pass before the title of teacher is deserved. And they are years of hard, unremitting work, of constant study, of reading and consulting, before proficiency in the particular subject or subjects is reached. Therefore, should not a teacher be looked up to for this hard-earned proficiency? Should not the pupils of such a teacher do all in their power to progress and succeed? Yet how often is the teacher vexed and harassed by lack of concentration, by inattention, and by carelessness in pupils? How often do pupils misuse the time allotted to special teachers and allow the blame for their failure to advance rest upon the teacher? These pupils of special teachers are usually of an age of responsibility, when they can understand the viewpoint of others—and can realize the difficulties of teaching. Should they not then determine to do credit to their teachers by putting forth every effort to succeed?

The relationship between teacher and pupil should be one of sympathy and understanding. The teacher should work for the pupil's good. He should give of his very best for the pupil's benefit and betterment. He should study the individual, for no two students can be treated alike either personally or pro-

---

Perfection should be the aim of every true artist.—*Beethoven*.

fessionally. He should endeavor to understand youth, which is ever impatient of correction, impatient of attainment and sensitive in spirit. He should foster carefully the spirit of emulation which is strong in every individual, and especially strong in young people, by being even-tempered, just, forbearing and perfectly sure of whatever he does.

And the pupil—how shall he meet his teacher? First, by acknowledging the teacher's superior knowledge and attainment, for there is no one so exasperating as the pupil who says— "Oh, yes, I knew that!" He should be respectful and attentive, persevering in the face of difficulties, constant in his application to his work, and, very important, prompt in his attendance to his lessons. He should accept correction meekly, for he should be eager to learn. In taking corrections, he should always remember that his teacher knows more than himself—and that if his mistakes are not set right he cannot make any headway. A teacher who conscientiously and painstakingly corrects his pupil's mistakes is a better teacher than one who gives indiscriminate praise. Does not even the Bible say, "Better are the rebukes of a friend than the kisses of an enemy"? Certainly the teacher wants to see his pupils advance and succeed, for otherwise there is no credit to either of them. The pupil will surely find that the teacher who points out his mistakes and insists upon their correction, is far more sincere and reliable than the one who invariably "pats him on the back" and says, "very good". The pupil must not expect to do the impossible. His teacher cannot learn for him, neither can he teach him, however clever they both may be, to reach perfection or proficiency in six lessons. "There is no royal road to learning" and the teacher is not to be blamed if progress is at first slow and doubtful.

A teacher knows the difference between a good pupil and an indifferent one—but how is a student to tell a teacher of merit from a charlatan? A teacher who makes a study of individual pupils, who puts personality into his work, is pretty apt to be a good teacher. And as results are accounted fair proof—the teacher who has succeeded with many and various kinds of pupils is sure to be a good teacher. Many benefits accrue from the selection of a good teacher at the beginning of study. There is the continued intercourse, constant growth of knowledge and understanding of each other's ways and

---

If you want enemies, excel others: if you want friends, let others excel you.—*Colton.*

methods; there is the one method of teaching which does away with the many changes from the methods of one teacher to the methods of another, which is the lot of so many unfortunate students; there is the steadiness of advancement, with no loss of time and effort through changing of teachers; and finally, and not least, there is the personal benefit of continued and pleasant association, of growth of affection and esteem, in short —of real friendship between the teacher and pupil.

Art has no fatherland, and all that is beautiful ought to be prized by us, no matter what clime or region has produced it.—*Weber*.

CHAPTER VI

WIND INSTRUMENT PLAYING FROM A HYGIENIC VIEWPOINT

While it may not be generally known, it is a matter of statistics that wind instrument players are, as a class, long-lived. It is also a physiological fact that correct breathing is one of the largest factors in maintaining the health of the body. So it is a logical conclusion to put these two facts together, and further to prove how and why wind instrument playing is decidedly a healthful and healthgiving exercise.

To begin with, the first thing we need to sustain our life is oxygen, which is taken into the body with the air we breathe. The more oxygen we breathe the clearer our blood, the stronger our circulation, and consequently the greater our vitality and strength in all directions. And since it is necessary to obtain as much oxygen as possible, it is imperative that we breathe properly. Wind instrument playing compels correct breathing. How many people have ever stopped to consider whether or not they know how to breathe, or if a few lessons in breathing would not be helpful? How many hundreds of cornet players and students are there who look back at the time when they took short, insufficient breaths, and quickly got out of breath; who now breathe deeply and easily and have an endurance before undreamed of, whose chests have expanded from one to three inches as the results of playing a wind instrument and of breathing properly?

Many children, both boys and girls, who were undersized for their ages, have been advised by their physicians to take up the study of a wind instrument for the development of their chests and lungs, and have attained splendid size and health as a direct result. People with weak lungs—even those unfortunate enough to have been threatened with, or actually suffering from tuberculosis of the lungs—have, either through medical or other professional advice, taken up a wind instru-

---

Music may be termed the universal language of mankind, by which human feelings are made equally intelligible to all.—*Liszt.*

ment, and, after varying periods of practice, in part or altogether conquered the weakness which sapped their strength,
and become healthy, strong men and women, able to take up
their duties and perform them. It is another statistically proven
fact that consumption or other lung troubles among wind instrument players are rare.

The third actual achievement of wind instrument practice
is the strengthening of the muscles. Not only are the muscles
of the mouth and face made firm, smooth and healthy, but the
wrists and arms become strong too. Also indirectly, the muscles
of the neck, shoulders and back have all these good effects
transmitted to them. And, of course, it can readily be seen
that since the playing of wind instruments strengthens and expands the lungs, it must also work to the same good purpose
upon the chest muscles.

Fourthly, there is no nerve strain in playing a wind instrument. When once the student is over the first idea (which of
course is a wrong idea) that he must exert all his power to blow
a tone into the instrument, he cannot but realize how little
effort is required to produce a tone. His teacher will at once
tell him "The easier you take it, the better your tone will be!"
And then it is no strain at all. No waste of nervous energy or
of physical force is necessary. Many women, many children,
and many elderly men, play wind instruments, and derive only
benefit and pleasure from it. Many men of over sixty years
are earning their livings by playing wind instruments, and are,
at the same time, strong, alert, and well, and enjoying life to
its fullest. In nearly every kind of institution it is possible to
think of, bands are formed and maintained, composed solely of
the inmates, with the direct result of more pleasure, more happiness, incentive to do something, and finally and happily, more
and better health.

Think more of your own progress than of the opinion of others.—*Mendelssohn.*

CHAPTER VII

THE BENEFITS OF ENSEMBLE PLAYING

Many who perform on musical instruments do not realize the importance of ensemble playing, and the benefits that may be derived therefrom. It makes no difference what instrument one plays, he should endeavor to play with others who perform on the same or different instruments. One's musicianship cannot possibly be considered complete without one's having had the benefit of this necessary experience. Those who do not play with others are missing much that is beautiful, instructive, interesting and satisfying.

The only instruments that are complete in themselves are the piano and organ, because they can produce both the necessary melody and harmony. Other instruments are merely instruments of melody, and nothing can be more monotonous and uninteresting than to hear one instrument alone, playing melody continually. The most beautiful melodies ever written would not be effective if they were not well harmonized. It is in the harmonization more than in anything else that the composer shows his skill. Any person can invent a melody.

If ensemble playing is cultivated, the performers will broaden their musical knowledge and understanding in numerous ways. First of all, it improves the ear. It helps one to secure perfect control of his instrument, in regard to moderation of tone, etc. It gives a better and more complete idea of the importance of time and rhythm. It will tend more than anything else to make one play the music precisely as it is written, and without the exaggeration in which many soloists indulge. It gives one a knowledge of other instruments, and a better idea of other combinations of sounds and effects.

In playing alone, a performer can play wrong continually without ever detecting it, but in ensemble playing, unless the instruments harmonize and play precisely together, even an unmusical person can readily detect the faults. Now the question

---

Any fool can play fast, but it takes a good musician to play slowly.—*Anon.*

22

arises "With what other instrument should one play?" This query is easily answered. First of all, solos are written for every instrument imaginable with piano accompaniment, and every instrumentalist should have a repertoire of solos of this description. Playing with the piano is always satisfying because the harmony is complete and gives a good, solid background to the solo instrument. Players of wind instruments in particular should play with the piano as often as possible.

The performer should strive to play ensemble music of all kinds, duets, trios, quartets, etc., and should try to play in some good orchestra and band. Players of all wind instruments will gain much by organizing trios, or quartets. They will be surprised and delighted to ascertain to what extent their playing will be improved, and what a variety of effects may be obtained by the cultivation of ensemble playing. There are players in every community, and suitable music can be secured for almost any combination of instruments.

Music is a discipline, and a mistress of order and good manners.—*Martin Luther.*

PART II

CHAPTER VIII

INSTRUMENTS OF THE BAND

The modern Concert Band is an institution which should command the serious consideration of all those interested in any way in music. Composers of the past have practically ignored the band despite the fact that most of them wrote music in all other forms, and for almost every known combination of instruments. As a result of the neglect of the composers, the band has never had a repertoire of its own. Many composers of the present generation, however, have realized that the band is worthy of consideration, and have written for it. Percy Grainger in a letter to me in 1920, after he and Victor Herbert had (as judges in a contest) selected the best original compositions for band, wrote as follows: "After having studied the assemblage of compositions for Band sent in to your prize competition, I have no hesitation in considering the work "A Chant from the Great Plains" (motto "Dum spiro, spero") as outstandingly deserving of the prize, in my opinion; as this composition not only displays a wider range of creative gifts and a more emotional expressiveness than any of the others, but also treats the subtle tonal palette of the Band with a very sensitive appreciation of its varied possibilities. This seems to me very important, since such a band as that organized and directed by you is in many respects, the equal if not the superior of the best symphony orchestra for the expression of many phases of modern music and modern emotionality, and it is most desirable that composers shall use these potentialities to the full."

Percy Grainger is one of our present day composers who has shown a great interest in the development of bands and has already written a number of compositions for them. He understands the band thoroughly through first-hand experience, having served in one of the American bands, as an actual player, for

---

The human voice is really the foundation of all music.—*Richard Wagner.*

a considerable time during the war. He, like many other famous musicians of the present, realizes that the band offers more possibilities for study and experiment than the old masters ever dreamed. Dr. Carl Busch, the veteran composer, who, incidently, won the prize to which Percy Grainger referred, expressed himself recently as follows: "Hearing various bands on their visits to the West, strengthened my belief in the Concert Band, and created a desire to express myself through this medium. The very large apparatus at one's disposal, its manifold combinations and tone colors, showed clearly the possibility of new and interesting effects. The effort on the part of the American Bandmasters' Association to interest composers in this field, already now bearing fruit, is strongly to be commended. On the other hand, the Concert Band is still growing and will continue to grow; the last twenty years have witnessed an amazing development in leadership, 'bandstration' and technical perfection on the part of the individual players. Add to this, the advent of original compositions for band, and the outlook is exceedingly bright. My impression of the Concert Band as a medium for artistic expression, is therefore decidedly a favorable one." Dr. Carl Busch, like Percy Grainger, became so interested in bands and band music, that he, too, learned to play several wind instruments. He became interested in bands when, as a young man, he was a student in Paris. He helped earn his expenses by copying band parts from the full scores, for the well-known Garde Republicaine Band.

In the book "Music, a Science and an Art" by John Redfield, former lecturer on "Physics of Music", Columbia University, (published by Alfred A. Knopf) the author says:— "The Symphony Orchestra has perhaps reached a higher state of development in America than anywhere else. But the possibilities for further development inherent in the Concert Band, the great popularity it has attained in less than a hundred years and the tremendous present interest in the development and cultivation of bands and band music, all point unmistakably to the conclusion that the real Concert Band in the comparatively near future, will reach a position of musical respectability and artistic excellence, at least equal to the Symphony Orchestra, and perhaps *superior* to it."

That the band has a future is definite. Its progress was for years retarded in many ways, the principal reason being

---

Music is a heavenly art; nothing supplants it except true love.—*Berlioz.*

that it has never had a standardized instrumentation such as the orchestra has had. The instrumentation varies in every country and in the individual countries themselves there is no official instrumentation.

The Band is composed of three distinct sections, the Reed, (or Woodwind), Brass, and Percussion. Below I shall give a composite list of instruments that are used in bands of the various countries. Later on in this chapter a list of the instruments used in our modern American Bands will be given.

This composite list is intended to give an idea of the large variety of instruments that are available for band purposes and that are or have been in use until recently in the various bands of the world.

Reed and Woodwind Instruments

Piccolos in Db, C	Bb Soprano Saxophone
Flutes in C, Db	Eb Alto Saxophone
Oboe	Bb Tenor Saxophone
Cor Anglais (English Horn)	Bb Baritone Saxophone
Ab Clarinet	Bb Bass Saxophone
Eb Clarinet	Eb Soprano Sarrusophone
Bb Clarinet	Bb Soprano Sarrusophone
Eb Alto Clarinet	Eb Alto Sarrusophone
Bb Bass Clarinet	Bb Tenor Sarrusophone
Contra Bass Clarinet	Eb Baritone Sarrusophone
Bassethorn	Bb Bass Sarrusophone
Bassoon	Eb Contra Bass Sarrusophone
Contra Bassoon	C Contra Bass Sarrusophone
Heckelphone	Bb Contra Bass Sarrusophone

Saxophones and Sarrusophones are made of Brass, but they belong to the Reed Section in view of the fact they are played with reeds.

There are two types of Reed Instruments,—those played with Double Reeds and those played with Single Reeds. The Double Reeds include the Oboes, English Horns, Bassoons, and Sarrusophones. Single Reed Instruments include all Clarinets and all Saxophones.

Life seems to go on without effort, when I am filled with music.—*George Eliot*

The Brass Instruments comprise the following:

Eb Horns	Tenor Horns
F Horns	Euphoniums
F and Bb Horns (Double Horn)	Bb Bass Fluegelhorns
Eb Alto Horns	Tenor Trombones
Eb Mellophone	Bass Trombones
Bb Cornets	Eb Tubas
Eb Cornets	Bb Tubas
Bb Fluegelhorns	C Tubas
Bb Trumpets	F Tubas
Eb Trumpets	BBb Tubas
Baritone (Althorn)	CC Tubas

The Percussion Instruments include the following:

Tympani	Cymbals
Bass Drums	Xylophones
Small Drums	Bells

and a large variety of Traps of all descriptions for various effects.

In addition to the above, many of the large Concert Bands also include:

1 or 2 Harps	String Basses

The above list shows what instruments are or have been used in bands throughout the world. Some of these are now quite obsolete. Some of them have never been used in our American Bands. A few of them could be introduced with good effect. There are people who are interested in the band movement who seem anxious to put every type of wind instrument in the band,—everything that can be blown into. This would be a serious mistake. There are many wind instruments that are so similar in quality that they would be a detriment rather than an addition to the band.

In regard to Sarrusophones, it may be said that they are used frequently to replace Oboes and Bassoons, because the tonal qualities of these instruments are somewhat alike. If a band includes Oboes and Bassoons it hardly seems possible that Sarrusophones could add much, if anything, to the tonal coloring. As a matter of fact, they might clog up the quality and give it a muddy effect. The Eb Contra Bass Sarrusophone, however, is the most useful of the entire family and could be included in our American Bands to good effect. The Contra Bass Sarrusophone in C is used occasionally in Orchestras instead of the Contra Bassoon.

The origin of harmony is divinity.—*Pythagoras.*

The Heckelphone is an instrument which was made by Heckel at the request ·of Richard Strauss who wanted some unusual tonal effect in a certain part of his opera "Salome". The instrument has no particular value otherwise, and would not enhance the tonal quality of the band, except for some special effect. The Bassethorn was used in Russian Bands. It is very similar to the Alto Clarinet except that it is built in F.

The Ab Clarinet is never used in this country.

Eb Horns are rarely used in this country. Most French Horns are built in F and the Double Horns in F and Bb.

Eb Cornets are no longer used in America. They are used in England to a large extent in their purely Brass Bands, in which they serve to good advantage.

The proper use of the Cornet and Fluegelhorn is a very important matter. The Cornet is a modification of the Fluegelhorn and, I believe, an improvement over it. The quality of tone of these two instruments is so similar that it seems totally unnecessary to have both of them in a band. If there are Cornets, then Fluegelhorns are unnecessary—and vice versa. For some very special effect, and if a *special part* is written for the Fluegelhorn, it might be added in some instances to good effect, but it hardly seems necessary to include it in the regular instrumentation of a band.

The Eb Trumpet is not used in our bands, but it could be added with considerable advantage, as it would be a fine connecting link between the Cornets and Trumpets and the Trombones.

The Tenor Horn is also not used in our bands, much to our disadvantage. I believe it should be added. It would be very useful, and would help us to correct many mistakes in our arrangements of the past. In operatic music many of the vocal Tenor arias are given to the Euphonium or Baritone in band arrangements, and this is an inexcusable mistake. Although the Baritone is an instrument of smaller bore than the Euphonium, they are entirely too similar in tonal quality. In fact, in our American Bands absolutely no attention is paid to the difference between these two instruments. It seems to me that it would be much more important for our bands to include either a Tenor Horn and a Baritone,—or a Tenor Horn and a Euphonium. Then we could have a greater variety of tone, as well as a proper distribution of the parts in our band arrangements.

Music and love are the wings of the soul.—*Berlioz.*

The Bass Fluegelhorn is not used in our bands, and as it is so similar to the Baritone and Euphonium quality and register it would not add very much.

As to the Trombones, it is a mistake to have all three parts—first, second and third, played on instruments of the same size. The best and proper effect is obtained by having the first part played on small bore Trombones. The second part should be played on medium bore Trombones, and the third parts on real bass Trombones. If this is done, the effect will be improved at once.

With the Tubas or Basses, it is good to have a variety. Eb and BBb instruments produce a fine effect. CC Tubas are also very beneficial. Much of the success of the basses, however, depends upon the capabilities of the players, rather than on the particular type of instrument they use. String Basses add much to the quality of the brass basses for concert purposes. The tone of this instrument blends well with woodwinds. The "pizzicato" effect, too, is one which the Tubas cannot accomplish. The String Bass has a vibrating tone which makes itself felt even in fortissimo passages.

The Harp can be used to advantage when the composer has written an appropriate part for it. It should not be used to fill in at random.

It has been the custom of our American publishers in the past to publish editions according to the needs and requirements of the day. There was no standardized instrumentation. Years ago there were not very many bands other than the professional bands that were worthy of consideration. Times have changed. The publishers of today have to take the purely professional band into consideration scarcely at all, inasmuch as there are so very few of them left. There are thousands of High School Bands, College Bands, etc., many of which are as good as some of the professional ones. They are capable of playing the highest type of music, and it is to these bands that the publishers are turning most of their efforts.

The question of a Standard Instrumentation for Concert Bands has been given a great deal of careful study by the American Bandmasters' Association. A special committe was appointed to make a year's study of the subject. The report of this committee was submitted at the convention which took

---

Music must begin in harmony, continue in harmony and end in harmony.
—*Confucius.*

place in Boston, in April 1931, and was unanimously approved. The list as given below refers to the *edition of the music* rather than the number of players. Every capable bandmaster will, of course, know how many of each kind of instrument he must have to secure a proper balance of tone.

The report of the "Music and Instrumentation Committee", of the American Bandmasters' Association which was adopted at the Boston convention follows:

(Conductor (3 staves)
1st Flute in C
2nd Flute in C or C Piccolo
1st Oboe
2nd Oboe (and English Horn)
Eb Clarinet
1st Bb Clarinet
2nd Bb Clarinet
3rd Bb Clarinet
4th Bb Clarinet
Alto Clarinet
Bass Clarinet
1st Bassoon
2nd Bassoon
Soprano Saxophone in Bb (ad lib.)
1st Alto Saxophone in Eb
2nd Alto Saxophone in Eb
Tenor Saxophone in Bb
Baritone Saxophone in Eb
Bass Saxophone in Bb (ad lib.)
1st Horn in F
2nd Horn in F
3rd Horn in F

4th Horn in F
1st Alto in Eb
2nd Alto in Eb
3rd Alto in Eb
4th Alto in Eb
1st Cornet in Bb
2nd Cornet in Bb
1st Trumpet in Bb
2nd Trumpet in Bb
1st Trombone in Bass Clef
2nd Trombone in Bass Clef
3rd Trombone in Bass Clef
1st and 2nd Trombones in Treble Clef
Baritone in Treble Clef
Euphonium in Bass Clef
1st and 2nd Basses (printed together)
String Bass
Tympany (Xylophone, etc.)
Drums and Traps
Harp (ad lib.)
39 regular parts and 4 ad libitum parts

The instrumentation for Concert Bands, and the suggestions recommended by the American Bandmasters may not please everyone, but they are surely safe and sane. Naturally, in order to have a finely balanced band these suggestions need not be rigidly adhered to, but the basis of this instrumentation is sound and well-balanced, so that artistic results may be achieved. At least here is a good basis to work on. As time goes on slight changes may be made, and if they are, let us hope they will be for the better. The men who studied this question of Instrumentation for Concert Bands and those who argued the various points at the convention were among the best known and most experienced bandmasters in the United States and Canada.

Music is the essence of order and leads to all that is good, just and beautiful.
—*Plato.*

The Eb Clarinet is not used in our present day arrangements as prominently as it was in the past, and in fact, some of our best concert bands do not use this instrument at all. Mr. Sousa did not use it for many years, nor did I. This instrument has many advantages however if properly played. I have again added it to the instrumentation of my band.

Four clarinet parts are indicated in the list. Some editions call for four, but most arrangements for three.

The Soprano Saxophone part is an "ad libitum" part in view of the fact that the instrument is the most difficult of the Saxophone family, and few players have made a success of it. Bass Saxophone is also "ad lib.".

The two sets of Horn parts are printed in some of the large concert editions so that those young bands who still have Eb instruments will be spared the transposing.

If a composer wishes to write three cornet parts and two trumpet parts, or vice versa, there is no reason why he should not do so. But there should be cornets and trumpets in every band. The band which has only trumpets cannot possibly be considered first class, or correct.

As to smaller bands, much of the music arranged for the instrumentation above, could be used advantageously by smaller bands, if they are not too small and if the parts are well cued. However, in general, things arranged for large bands are not appropriate for small ones. There should in reality be special arrangements for large bands, and separate ones for small bands. This will allow them both to do justice to the music they perform. No composition can be arranged so that it will sound well with a band of seventy players, and equally well with a band of twenty. This is an impossibility. Some of our smaller bands, municipal bands, Army and Navy Bands, should be given special consideration. During my extensive travels I have heard several bands in small cities that did fine work indeed. Some of them were handicapped by the lack of good arrangements for small bands. In a few instances, where the leaders were good arrangers and were able to select other published arrangements that were suitable for their organizations, the results were very good.

Before ending this chapter, it seems that something should be said about the Eb Alto Horn. It is true that the instrument has been discarded, but I still believe it has value. As a matter

---

Music is the expression of a refined nature.—*Schumann.*

of fact, for Amateur Bands, I believe it is far more satisfactory, when French Horn players cannot be secured, than the Mellophone. The great trouble with the Alto Horn in the past was that few people ever played it well. The instrument has a nice tone. Eb Altos could also be used to good advantage in very large bands to augment the French Horn passages which may not come through prominently enough. This is done in some of the foreign bands. In my own band last year, I tried an experiment, and in all marches (especially American arrangements) where the French Horns are the only instruments playing the so-called afterbeats, I had Altos used. These particular Altos were made so that they could be played with the French Horn mouthpieces. French Horns cannot satisfactorily produce staccato afterbeats that come through properly and, therefore, a great deal of the "pep" and "punch" of a march is lost. My players rebelled at first, but when they became accustomed to it they soon saw what a difference it made in the rendition of a March. They were pleased then. The Altos were only used in the playing of Marches. French Horns come through better on longer notes. These particular Altos were built in F, since my players use F Horns, and were Bell-front models. For Marching purposes, surely the Alto can be used to better advantage than the French Horn. Bandmasters should give a thought to the Alto before discarding it entirely. It is a satisfactory and useful instrument if well played. The all-Brass Bands of England use Altos to the exclusion of French Horns because they balance better with the other brasses. Naturally this would be more apparent in a strictly brass ensemble.

SILVER CLARINETS, ETC.

Before concluding this important chapter the subject of Silver Clarinets should be discussed. During the past few years, many players have adopted the Silver (or other metal) Clarinet in preference to that of wood. These instruments will be found to predominate in many of the amateur bands, and many professional players are also using them at present. At first there was a general prejudice against these Silver Clarinets, just as there was against the Silver Flute at the start, yet today the Wooden Flute has become almost obsolete amongst professionals.

It's the songs you sing and the smiles you wear that make the sunshine everywhere.

Last year a test was made by the clarinet section of my band, and certain passages were played first on the Silver Clarinets and then the wooden—and vice-versa. The most experienced musicians (who acted as judges) could not tell which type of instrument was being played. Thus it is proven that the Silver instrument which is carefully made will prove as satisfactory in intonation, and tonal quality as the one of wood. In fact—a finely made Silver instrument may possibly have some advantages. It will not warp—it can be made in one piece —and its mechanism is apt to be more accurate and responsive.

Personally—I am of the opinion—that in the near future, we will no longer have a real "Wood Section" in our bands and orchestras. Wood Flutes are practically out of date. Silver (or other metal) Clarinets are rapidly coming to the fore, and it is my belief that it will not be long before Oboes and Bassoons of silver (or other metal) will come into common use. When that time comes the so-called "Wood Section" or *"Reed Section"* will be a mere name—or a memory.

While on this subject, I should like to quote a few paragraphs of a letter received recently from my friend Georges Barrere, the eminent flutist.

"Silver flutes were first introduced by Theobald Boehm in 1847. But this doesn't mean that silver flutes were played then. In Europe, I think France was the first country to have the silver flute used generally. My first teacher used it many years before I came to him. Henry Altes, teacher at the Paris Conservatoire used the silver flute exclusively and so did all his pupils since about the year 1870, if not earlier. England followed; Germany and Italy being much more conservative. In fact wood flutes are still in honor, especially in Italy.

In America, when I came in 1905, very few silver flutes were used, except in the Boston Symphony where Jacquet played before 1890, then Andre Maquarre and every one thereafter. In New York my predecessor in the N. Y. Symphony, Charles Mole, was playing silver, but was nearly the only one in the city. Wm. S. Haynes, flute manufacturer of Boston, claims that in 1905 when I came, he used to make one silver against 100 wooden ones, while now he estimates that he makes one wood flute against 100 silver ones. This will edify you on the popularity of the silver instrument. When I say silver I mean metal, because cheap instruments are made of maillechort

Music is well said to be the speech of angels.—*Carlyle.*

(German silver) silver plated, while prosperous artists and even myself use Gold Flutes.

The silver Clarinets seem to have the same advantages as the silver Flutes, but are long in taking their place. The reason is that the makers are unable to correct the shortcomings of all clarinets, and players blame the metal, whereas they should consider that the slight corrections they can make upon the imperfection of any clarinet are the result of long experience. Oboes in Silver have been made in Germany and met with success. Why they are not popular might be because of the high cost of such new model of instrument. Bassoons have been tried in aluminum; but are still in the state of experiment. I am very much in favor of silver Clarinets, even as they are today. I never heard oboes or bassoons other than wood; but it is needless to say that bassoons can be improved in so many ways that we shall welcome experiment towards that aim. Metal might be one."

The hardest trial of the heart is whether it can bear a rival's failure without triumph.—*Aikin.*

JOHN PHILIP SOUSA AND EDWIN FRANKO GOLDMAN

CHAPTER IX

COMPARISON OF THE BAND AND ORCHESTRA
SHOULD THE BAND PLAY ORCHESTRAL MUSIC?

Bands are still in their infancy, even though great progress has been made, especially in the last few years. Bands and band music are not generally understood, and therefore, both are frequently misjudged. There are many who look down upon bands, and consider them inferior to orchestras. The band is *not* inferior to the orchestra. It is simply *different*. Each can achieve certain effects which the other cannot. We might say that the orchestra is feminine, and the band masculine, although the band can be extremely gentle and mild. A band can give as artistic a performance as an orchestra. A fine symphony orchestra consists of fine performers, experienced musicians who are well trained. A fine band likewise must be made up of fine players who are well drilled.

Patrick Sarsfield Gilmore once said—"With the Band, there is *life, vim, dash, vigor, brilliance,* a *something* which stirs the blood, a *virile strength* that cannot be produced by an orchestra, no matter how superbly it plays. A first-class Band is like a *perfect gentleman, strong, masterful, kingly,* yet *kind, tender* and *true.* The orchestra contains as virtues—*beauty, grace, sentiment, pathos, constancy* and *allurement,* in the femine manner."

Bands are too frequently judged by fourth rate street parade bands. I do not wish to belittle such bands, but it is a fact, that most bands of that type do not rehearse, and, of course, they are not made up of good players. They consist of what we might term "musical jobbers," who make a business of music, but who are not interested in it as an art. The future will eliminate such "jobbers" for there is only to be room for real musicians and real performers in the new scheme of things.

Many people, particularly those who patronize symphony concerts and who are prejudiced against bands, have never heard a really fine Concert Band. Many of them shudder at the

---

Music loosens a heart that care has bound.—*Byrd.*

word "band." They seem to feel that there is no reason for the existence of a band except for military or marching purposes. They will listen to a symphony orchestra, a chorus, a string-quartet, piano and violin recitals, etc., but turn an absolutely cold shoulder to the band. Why? If orchestras, choruses, and string quartets can perform artistically, why can't a band? It must be admitted that there have been many bad bands in the past, but there have been bad orchestras too. There are those who feel that the band is a mere "noise-maker." There have been such bands and some of them are in existence today, but a good band is a fine medium for artistic expression of the best that the art of music has to offer. The true music lover should appreciate and encourage any type of ensemble music that is artistically and creditably performed. Even some of our music critics have not shown the slightest interest in bands and band music, or in the advancement of them.

The youth of our land is being trained musically. Every school, every high school, every college, practically every orphan asylum has its band. Institutions of all kinds, many large business concerns, fraternal organizations such as the Masons, Elks, various branches of the American Legion, have their bands. They do *not* all have orchestras, so it will readily be seen that bands predominate. One particular thing that the band has in its favor is the fact that it is far more spectacular than the orchestra. Most bands wear uniforms, and this, together with their bright, shiny instruments make for a fine and attractive appearance.

These thousands of bands in our country are, what we might call "Concert Bands." Most bands of the past were known as "military bands" because they performed military duties. They paraded at the head of their regiments. Their music marked the rhythm to which the soldiers marched. They inspired the soldiers to greater deeds of valor in war. Let us hope that these strictly "military bands" will soon have no military duties and that wars will be a thing of the past. What we want is the Concert Band. The concert band, as instituted in this country by Partick Sarsfield Gilmore and John Philip Sousa, is the type of organization that is being sponsored in every city in the United States today. We need and want better bands. Every child should be given the opportunity of learning music for the cultural advantages that it offers.

A song will outlive all sermons in the memory.—*Giles.*

Who would have thought twenty-five years ago that our High School Bands would ever be able to perform the works of the great masters, Bach, Beethoven, Wagner, etc.? Who would have believed that youngsters in the primary grades would be able to perform creditably on such difficult instruments as the Oboe, Bassoon, French Horn, Tympani, Harp, etc.? Yet, practically all of our high school bands and even many of our primary school bands, particularly those of the West, and Middle West, besides having a large number of members, are perfect in their instrumentation. The layman can scarcely realize what this means.

The one great drawback to bands is the fact that most of the music which they perform is music that was originally composed for orchestra. It has to be specially arranged or transcribed in order that bands may perform it. In the past, this has not always been done artistically or successfully, but some remarkably fine arrangements have been made. At the suggestion of the American Bandmasters' Association, many of the defects and obstacles of the past are being remedied. The publishers are bringing out finer arrangements, better editions, and a greater variety of suitable compositions. In other words, the standard is being raised considerably.

John Philip Sousa made the following comparison between the Band and the Orchestra: "The orchestra has had a decided advantage over the wind band, because from the time of Haydn, the father of the orchestra, up to the present time, its orchestration has not changed. Every addition to the orchestra has been with one exception, a wind instrument. The exception has been the introduction of the Harp. The Military Band has a different instrumentation in every country and no doubt it has been the victim of political chicanery and very seldom the child of music. In every country—England, France, Holland, Austria, etc., it has been the plaything to suit some men in their idea of what a military band should be. The orchestra, whether playing light music or music of a heavier sort, simply plays it with the instruments traditionally used, either from a symphonic standpoint or a so-called popular one—but not so with the band.

The band has been circumscribed in its music and it is a common expression among musicians to say 'that piece is not suited for band'; that is true only in a few instances, and such pieces, where the string instruments are paramount, should

---

Music is a more lofty revelation than all wisdom and philosophy.—*Beethoven.*

not be essayed by the band. One of the objects of the newly formed society of bandmasters (American Bandmasters' Association) is to bring about a oneness of band arrangements among the nations. Today, a composition arranged for orchestra is just as feasible whether played in France or Spain, in England or in America, in Germany or in Austria—but not so with the band. Every country has a different instrumentation for a band, and the same orchestration for an orchestra."

Grove's Dictionary says: "In fact, the present Orchestra is becoming a large *Wind Band*, plus strings, instead of a String Band plus Wind." The actual difference between a band and orchestra is that a band is composed entirely of wind, (woodwinds and Brasses) and percussion instruments, (although many of our concert bands include String Basses and Harps) whereas the orchestra is composed of Strings, Woodwinds, Brasses and Percussion. The orchestra is over two hundred years old, while the Concert Band started about sixty years ago.

There are some who still believe the band has no right to perform music that was written for the orchestra. If that be true, then the orchestra too should perform only music that was originally scored for it. The present-day Concert Band is a young and modern institution and is vastly different in character, style and ideals from the old military band whose sphere of usefulness was limited. The Concert Band has an adequate instrumentation and a large variety of instruments. It is capable of giving adequate and artistic performances of practically all classical and modern music. If, for example, such composers as Wagner, Tchaikowsky, Richard Strauss, Saint-Saens, Verdi, Puccini, Gounod, Ravel, Rimsky-Korsakow, Respighi, and other famous masters had felt that their music was being mutilated by band performance, would they have permitted their own publishers to issue arrangements and transcriptions for band?

The same applies to other famous composers whose works have been transcribed. Only recently, the firm of Durand in Paris brought out a band arrangement of "Bolero" by Ravel.

Give us, O give us the man who sings at his work! He will do more in the same time—he will do it better—he will persevere longer. One is scarcely sensible of the fatigue whilst he marches to music. The very stars are said to make harmony as they revolve in their spheres. Wondrous is the strength of cheerfulness, altogether past calculation its powers of endurance. Efforts, to be permanently useful, must be uniformly joyous, a spirit all sunshine, graceful from very gladness, beautiful because bright.—*Carlyle.*

This arrangement was made in America by Mayhew Lester Lake for the Goldman Band. It was sent to Paris and approved by Ravel, and, as a matter of fact, he was so pleased with it that the French firm bought the arrangement and published it. Of course, orchestral music does not sound precisely the same when played by a band, but it can still be beautiful with a different tonal coloring. As mentioned before, bands and orchestras are different in their medium of expression, and both can achieve different and artistic effects if the conductor is a capable one.

A few years ago Leopold Stokowski organized a band of one hundred players and gave concerts each Spring for several seasons. He had made special arrangements of works by Bach and other masters. In fact, he made some of the arrangements himself. He said, at the time, that he never realized what wonderful results could be achieved with a band, and that conducting one was more inspiring than conducting an orchestra. Did he desecrate Bach? Men like Toscanini have the highest regard for good bands, and they do not look down upon them. They realize that bands can play artistically. It is safe to say that many works which were written for orchestra sound better and more effective when played by band.

Much of the Bach music which we hear today for symphony orchestra was originally written for the organ, yet it sounds beautiful in its arrangement for the orchestra. How many hundreds of these great organ works by Bach have been arranged by other famous musicians and composers for orchestra! Much Bach music has also been arranged for band. Why not? Has not the band the same privileges? As a matter of fact many of these compositions sound even better for band than for orchestra, because every musician will agree that the band can achieve better organ effects than the orchestra. Bach wrote several sonatas for Violin alone and some of these have been arranged for string quartet, string orchestra, etc. The famous Bourree by Bach (from a Sonata for violin alone) was arranged by Saint-Saens for the piano. It has also been transcribed in a dozen other forms. Handel did not write his world-famous "Largo" as an orchestral piece. It was composed as a vocal solo in one of his operas, yet how many times is this number sung? It gained its greatest fame as an orchestral composition, or as a violin solo. It has been re-arranged and transcribed in a hundred different ways, yet who finds objections to this?

It is much easier to be critical than to be correct.—*D'Israeli.*

How about the thousands of piano solo arrangements of Bach—and other great masters, whose works were written for organ and other instruments? In the case of the organ, the band comes nearer to giving the actual effects than any other musical medium.

Last year a number of "letter writers" wrote to the New York papers complaining that the Goldman Band should not be permitted to perform the music of the masters, as all great works were written for orchestra. The writers were positive that the band was desecrating these works. The writers showed by their letters, however, that they did not know what instruments the band consisted of. One of the writers went on to say that with his own eyes he saw two men using hammers or mallets to beat on steel bars to make a noise in the finale of Tchaikowsky's "1812" Overture. This proved that bands made more noise than music. He also saw the bass drummer pounding on his drum with all his power. This letter writer did not realize that the steel bars were chimes, representing the ringing of the church chimes at Moscow in celebration of the Russian victory over the French in 1812, and that the composer wanted a large variety of them used. The letter writer did not realize that the bass drum beats were supposed to be cannon-shots to describe the battle, and that Tchaikovsky called for actual cannon shots in the score! Symphony orchestras sometimes have used real cannons. What would this letter writer have said if we had used cannons? In the original score for orchestra, the composer calls for chimes, cannons, and a brass band to reenforce the orchestra. Letter writers from time to time have done their utmost to defame the band, but they have generally shown that they had more time than knowledge and that, in many instances, they were publicity seekers. As Disraeli said "It is much easier to be critical than to be correct." One of these letter writers went so far as to say that the huge audiences that attended the band concerts to hear Beethoven, Wagner, Tchaikovsky, etc., were not real music lovers. He noticed, so he said, that the harmonic structure of the band arrangements was different from the orchestral versions, as if any real musician would ever dare change the harmonies of the masters. He heard this, however, with his "super ears." He was prejudiced against bands or else had some other complaint. At least he had to let the world know just what *he* thought.

Those who bring sunshine into the lives of others cannot keep it from themselves.
—*J. M. Barrie.*

At a concert a few years ago, one of my soloists sang "Elizabeth's Prayer" from Wagner's "Tannhaüser," and at the conclusion of the concert, a man (a Wagner enthusiast) came up to the bandstand and told me how much he had enjoyed the performance. He felt, however, that the accompaniment to this aria had lost considerably through the transcription for band. He did not realize that we played the number precisely as Richard Wagner wrote it, because in the opera itself, this aria is accompanied throughout only by wood-wind instruments. What the real musician looks for is an artistic performance and if he gets that, he is generally pretty well satisfied. The layman is often too critical without possessing the knowledge of facts. "A little knowledge is a dangerous thing."

Orchestras frequently feature Liszt's many Hungarian Rhapsodies, yet they were written for the Piano. Most of them are more inspiring, however, when played in their orchestral coloring. Johann Strauss first wrote his famous "Blue Danube" Waltz as a choral number, and when it proved a dismal failure in that form, it was re-written for orchestra and took the world by storm. How many great composers, *themselves*, have written something in one particular form and re-arranged or transcribed it for another instrument or other combinations of instruments?

Those who claim that the band has no right to perform music originally written for orchestra have a weak argument indeed. We might as well say that a book or play written in one language should not be translated into another. If Wagner's music does not sound adequate for band, then Shakespeare's "Othello" does not sound adequate in German.

It must be admitted that the great composers of the past did not write for band, and that the band has not, in the past, had a repertoire of its own; but this is being changed now. Through the influence of the American Bandmasters' Association some of the foremost composers of the world are now writing original works directly for band. Ottorino Respighi, the great Italian master, has composed a Symphonic Poem for band; Gustave Holst, the famous English composer, also has written a new and wonderful work. Percy Grainger, Henry Hadley, Leo Sowerby, Carl Busch, Albert Roussel are others who have recently written worthwhile compositions for this medium. Maurice Ravel has promised to do likewise. Composers have

The man who disparages music as a luxury and non-essential is doing the nation an injury. Music now more than ever before is a present national need. There is no better way to express patriotism than through music.—*Woodrow Wilson*.

been handicapped because of the difference in the instrumentation of bands in each country. The American Bandmasters' Associat'on at one of its recent conventions decided upon a standard instrumentation for our American Concert Bands. This organization is now endeavoring to bring about a *standard international band instrumentation*. This will require a long time, but it will undoubtedly be accomplished some day.

Bands must be considered on a par with other musical combinations. They *are* capable of artistic performances, and they should be judged solely on their merit. It should be remembered that most people heard their first music from a band. The band has created many music lovers for the orchestra. Bands must have made a wide appeal to the public, for were any orchestra conductors in the history of the world ever as universally popular and beloved as Gilmore and Sousa? These two band giants were known to music lovers and to laymen alike, young and old, in all parts of the world.

In conclusion, it should be once more emphatically stated that if composers felt that the band was not an artistic medium for the performance of their works, they would be the ones to object. There is ample place in the musical world for both the band and the orchestra. Each has its own sphere of usefulness, and each can render valuable service in spreading the gospel of good music.

Wouldst thou know if a people be well governed, if its laws be good or bad, examine the music it practices.—*Confucius*.

CHAPTER X
THE CONDUCTOR

Many people who listen to band or orchestra concerts are in total ignorance of the functions of the conductor. There are those who believe he is chosen or appointed because of his looks, or because of his grace, or perhaps because of his good taste in clothes. People of intelligence have asked me what the conductor really does. Why does he stand in front? They believe that the musicians are reading their music, playing it, without ever looking at him.

The band or orchestra becomes one great instrument in the hands of the conductor, just as the violin or piano is an instrument in the hands of any solo performer. The conductor plays on his instrument—the band or orchestra—just as he feels. He interprets according to his own personal understanding and his inspiration. Under the direction of a capable conductor each member of the band or orchestra loses his own individuality and becomes simply a part of the one big instrument which must respond to the will of the conductor. In other words, the individual players in any large ensemble group must necessarily submerge their individuality in order to secure the effects which the conductor desires to achieve. Just as any individual player knows what effects he wants to bring forth in the solo music he performs, so the conductor must know what effects are essential in his reading of a work.

Inasmuch as it requires many different instruments to make up the one big instrument, the orchestra or band, the successful conductor must have a fund of knowledge and experience. He must know the compass and register of each instrument, and be familiar with its tonal qualities, its peculiarities, its strong and weak points, and the various effects which can be obtained from it. He must have a feeling for tonal balance and tonal color combinations, must know when one instrument should predominate over another. He must familiarize himself

It is the nature of instrumental music in its highest form to express in sounds what is inexpressible in words.—*Richard Wagner.*

44

with the ideas and intentions of the composer, and endeavor to carry them out. In the matter of the music of the masters and other standard music he must adhere in a large degree to the traditional interpretations. He must have a good idea of the proper tempo of the music he renders, and not merely resort to guesswork. One of the prime requisites of a conductor is a fine sense of rhythm.

The conductor who is most spectacular and makes the greatest number of gestures, or the one who is most graceful, is not necessarily the best conductor. A conductor can only be judged by the results he achieves. The ideal conductor is not extravagant in his gestures, but each signal, each movement of his hands or arms should bring forth some response in the music. As a matter of fact, the actual work of the conductor is done in the rehearsal room. This is where all corrections are made, where all the individual members, and various sections are moulded into a harmonious unit. During the actual concert performance the audience hears the result of what has been accomplished at rehearsals, and at the concert the conductor simply guides his players. This is comparable to a person who has been practicing certain pieces for weeks and then plays them in public. The conductor is the performer, the band or orchestra the instrument. The conductor becomes responsible for the performance and interpretation.

To those who believe that the players never look at the conductor, let me say that in any first-class organization each and every player sees every move, every gesture, every facial expression of the conductor. They keep one eye on the music, and one on the conductor, as it were. In organizations where the performers are not familiar enough with the music to watch the conductor properly, the rendition is bound to suffer in many ways.

About the training of a conductor, there is much to be said. First of all, he should be a capable performer on some one instrument. He should have a knowledge of the history of music. He should be able to compose and arrange. He should have a knowledge of all instruments, both band and orchestra. He should be familiar with the works of the masters and other standard music. He should keep himself well informed on al musical subjects, should hear all new and worthwhile music. He should hear the conductors of authority conduct the works he intends to direct,

Music to the mind is as air to the body.—*Plato.*

and become familiar with the correct and traditional interpretations.

The most useful instrument for the conductor to play is, of course, the piano (or organ) but many of the world's greatest conductors have not been able to perform on this instrument. With the piano one can always have the complete harmony when playing over or studying the compositions to be performed.

Conductors who have been trained under the great conductors of the world through having played in Symphony or Grand Opera Orchestras, or fine Bands, have a great advantage over those who have not had the benefit of this particular type of training. The advantages of this kind of experience are many. It gives the would-be conductors the privilege of being in close contact with men of authority, and the opportunity to observe their methods. They learn how rehearsals are conducted. They are made to realize the meaning of the baton, and the handling of it. They get an idea of tonal coloring and tonal balance, which takes others much longer to achieve. They also become familiar with interpretations that are authentic and correct. If one has the other qualifications for becoming a good conductor, the experience of playing under famous conductors is worth a great deal. After all, a great part of the art of conducting is learned through observation, and is imbibed through the ears and the eyes. Among the famous conductors who had the benefit of orchestral experiences are Hans Richter (one of Wagner's favorite conductors, and a French Horn player), Anton Seidl (another famous Wagnerian conductor who played the Tympani), Arturo Toscanini, who played the Cello, Serge Koussevitzky, who played the Contra Bass, and Frederick Stock, who played the Viola.

Naturally, the ideal conductor must have experience and he must acquire it as the opportunity presents itself. A certain very special talent is required in a successful conductor. Many of the world's most famous composers and performers have lacked this talent for conducting. Many great composers have been unable to give a fine or adequate performance of their own compositions as conductors. The conducting talent is quite a rare one. The real conductor must be a person of magnetism, of personality. He must be able to convey his feelings, his intentions, to others. He must be able to communicate his enthusiasm and his moods to those who play under him as well as to those

---

Reverence the old, but meet the new also with a warm heart. Cherish no prejudice against names unknown to you.—*Schumann.*

who are listening. He must be a sort of commander. Besides having a thorough knowledge of the music he conducts, he must be possessed of taste, good judgement, feeling, a sense of rhythm, tonal balance, and must know the composer's intentions, which should be respected at all times. The inner workings, the the inner voices of the composition played must be carefully brought out and not superficially treated. In other words, the conductor must lead and not follow as is often the case.

The conductor must also possess other qualifications besides the purely musical ones. He must always be dignified in the discharge of his duties and particularly so on the concert platform. His attitude toward his players should be one of respect, as should his attitude toward his audience. Unless he commands the absolute respect of his men his performances will be lacking in certain essential qualities. The good-will of the players is a very essential item in the life of a conductor—just as the good-will of an audience is. Strict discipline and punctuality should mark all rehearsals as well as all concerts.

It has been said many times that no organization is greater than its conductor. An inferior organization will do far better work under a capable conductor—just as a fine organization will do poorer work under an inferior conductor.

There are many thousands of school and college bands and orchestras in the country today, and their advancement during the past few years has been phenomenal indeed. The greatest need of today in this great movement is capable conductors. The development of good conductors has not kept pace with this movement. As good conductors are developed our bands and orchestras will improve. The national school band and orchestra contests of the past few years have proven that where the conductor and teacher were efficient, the organizations were excellent. But it was found that many conductors did not have the slightest idea of the tempi or the traditional interpretation of the compositions which they rendered. In most instances there was no excuse for this inasmuch as many of these compositions can be heard over the radio, played by the leading symphony orchestras and bands, or could be procured on phonograph records, recorded by organizations of standing. Conductors who do not take advantage of every opportunity to correct their interpretations are a detriment to their organizations.

Beauty is visible harmony.—*Aristotle.*

In the past, many freak conductors have achieved a degree of success, not because the performances which they directed were of such high musical value, but because they amused certain listeners with their antics and their clowning. The long-haired conductor, who walked up a few steps when the band played a crescendo, and walked down again when they played a decrescendo—and who walked over to each player who had a few solo notes to play, and made gestures as though he himself were drawing the notes from the performer's instrument, is now a thing of the past. Such foolery might be acceptable as a burlesque, but real music lovers are disgusted rather than impressed by such buffoonery.

The serious conductor will try to achieve his effects with the least possible amount of effort. Of course, he will only get out of the performance what he puts into it. His beat should be firm, distinct and unmistakable. Unfortunately many conductors lack the very first principle of conducting, namely the art of beating time, which in reality is the easiest part of conducting. Many conductors do not regulate their beats so that they are even. It is necessary at times to give a long, broad sweep of the arms, in slow movements, and at other times a shorter and quicker beat. The fewer and simpler the gestures, the more readily the players will respond.

If a mistake of some kind occurs during a performance, as is bound to happen occasionally even in the best regulated bands, the conductor should not in any way attract the attention of the audience to it through his gestures or signals. He should wait until after the performance to correct it, or discuss it with the performer. The conductor must have absolute control of himself while on the stage. He must realize that from the moment he sets foot on the stage, he is the center of attraction. He should acknowledge applause in a dignified manner. He should be prompt in starting his program. In appearance he should be immaculate. And above all, he should be ready and willing to assume the responsibility for the making of his program, as well as for its interpretation.

In conclusion, I wish to say that the conductor has a position of great responsibility and consequently much to answer for, both to his players and to his audiences.

Take a music bath once or twice a week for a few seasons. You will find it is to the soul what a water bath is to the body. This elevates and tends to maintain tone to one's mind. Seek, therefore, every clean opportunity for hearing it. Let music be as much a part of a day's routine as eating or reading or working.
—*Oliver Wendell Holmes.*

There are some conductors who prefer to conduct without the aid of the wooden baton. This is a matter of preference. It makes little or no difference so long as the music is well rendered. Then, too, in several instances, conductorless orchestras have sprung up, but these have generally disappeared again. Of course, it is possible to perform certain types of music without a conductor, but only in a mechanical manner. The inspiration and warmth, and frequently the precision and rhythm would be lacking. Such music would be machine-like.

It can definitely be stated that there will be a great field in the future for capable conductors, of bands, orchestras, and choruses. The need for developing such conductors is urgent. It is to be hoped, too, that in the near future some of our American Symphony Orchestras will be conducted by Americans. Naturally, we want the very best conductors no matter from what country they come, but it seems a rather sad commentary that not one of our major orchestras is led by an American. Bands, on the contrary, have produced many world-famous conductors. Inasmuch as America has progressed musically to such a large degree during the last decade, let us hope that we will soon have in our midst conductors of such calibre that even our symphony orchestras will seek them.

After the beginnings of reading, writing, arithmetic and geography, music is of greater educational value than any other subject taught in the schools.
—*P. P. Claxton, Ph.D., United States Commission of Education.*

CHAPTER XI
REHEARSALS

Rehearsals are the most important factor in the proper development of bands, but, unfortunately, most organizations are not in the position, for one reason or another, to hold a sufficient number of rehearsals. The concert performance of any band simply reflects what has been accomplished at the rehearsals.

The professional bands are handicapped to a very large extent because of the fact that the musicians, in most instances, must be paid by the hour for all rehearsals. It is for this reason that so many professional bands are unable to give creditable performances. For instance, if a professional band is engaged to give a concert, the cost is generally calculated at so much per man for the concert, and so much per man (extra) for the rehearsal. What is the result? In most instances those paying for the concert decide to pay for the concert, without a rehearsal. Such a concert is always disastrous. If our professional bands were engaged by the year, or for long seasons, so that they could build up a large and varied repertoire, they would be able to give a concert here and there without an extra rehearsal. Bands playing together steadily build up an ensemble of performance, but there are few professional bands in the United States that play together for more than a few weeks at a time.

To my mind, one of the reasons that professional bands have been treading the down-hill path for so many years, is the fact that most, or practically all, of the concert dates, and other engagements which they secure, are played without rehearsal. This is musical suicide. Another one of the very bad features is that most of these bands have so few dates that they have no regular personnel. If the leader or manager secures a date he goes to the headquarters of the Musical Union and engages whatever players are available, and when another date is procured he does the same, but does not always secure the same

---

Every trained youth and girl ought to be taught the elements of music early and accurately.—*Ruskin.*

players. It seems to me that it is not fair to give a concert performance at any time, or at any place, without a rehearsal. It is not fair to the musicians, nor is it fair to the audience. What some of these professional bands have perpetrated in the past is beyond description.

Many cities appropriate sums of money each year for open-air summer band concerts, but how many of the bands do any rehearsing for them? The City of New York, for instance, has appropriated from fifty thousand dollars to over a hundred thousand dollars at various times for seasons of summer concerts in the various parks. But there is no preparation for these concerts, no rehearsing, because there is no budget for rehearsals. This is indeed a sad state of affairs. This same method is pursued in many other cities, including Boston. In New York most of the bands are too small, and with their lack of a sufficient instrumentation and lack of rehearsals, are not in a position to reflect credit upon the cause of bands and band music. This lack of rehearsals is one of the great tragedies of the band. I firmly believe that the time will come when every important band engagement will include a rehearsal, without extra pay. It may be necessary to raise the concert pay of the musicians in order to do this, or now that adjustments are being made in all types of businesses and professions, perhaps our Unions will, instead of lowering the pay of musicians, include a free rehearsal. Something must be done to make it possible for professional bands to rehearse. Otherwise band engagements will become even fewer than at the present time, if such a thing is possible. Professional bands have lost ground. They must strive for a standard in order to be recognized again. Times are no longer what they were twenty years ago, and nothing mediocre will now suffice.

To prove the value of rehearsals, let us see what can be achieved through care and constant practice. Two years ago I went to hear a *brass* band which was engaged for the Canadian National Exhibition at Toronto, Canada. The band consisted of about twenty-four players. I had heard so much about English Brass Bands that I made this long trip in order to see and hear for myself. The band was made up entirely of brasses, and the players were all men who worked in mines. It hardly seemed possible that they could show good results as performers. Instead of remaining for a part of one concert

Where words fail, music speaks.—*Hans Christian Anderson.*

as I intended, I remained for three days. What this band achieved was a revelation to me. I was thrilled. It wasn't that these men individually were artists, for they were not, but their remarkable ensemble playing, their phrasing, tonal balance, and intonation was something long to be remembered. Their success could only be attributed to one thing—rehearsals and plenty of them. They rehearsed year in and year out, almost daily. Their conductor was a real drillmaster, who knew how to secure the effects he desired. Now, if a band composed of coal miners can reach such artistic heights, what could some of our professional bands do, with the proper amount of rehearsing? Our large cities all have many fine wind instrument players, men who have been carefully trained and who have had experience. If in each one of these cities a concert band were formed and regular rehearsals held throughout the year under the direction of a capable conductor, still greater results could be obtained, and more quickly, than those achieved by this band of miners. We would soon have super-bands. Wind instrument players must get together for the good of the cause of music, and be ready and willing to rehearse in order to achieve artistic results. Only in such a manner will the interest in professional bands be revived. The Musical Unions will do all in their power to help this cause, or else professional bands cannot thrive.

As for amateur bands, it must be said that the progress made by the High School and College Bands has been phenomenal indeed. These bands generally rehearse once a week, which, of course, is not sufficient. The bands that rehearse oftener reflect it in their playing, provided they have a competent conductor. The amateur rehearsal is a very different proposition from the professional. The professional player is supposed to be proficient on his instrument, and a good sight reader. Many of the amateur band players are beginners who have had little or no private instruction. The leader generally has to teach all the various instruments at the rehearsal, besides trying to get some ensemble work done. Leaders of these bands have a trying task indeed, but many of them get remarkable results. The leader who is capable and has a sufficient number of rehearsals naturally makes the best showing at his performances.

One of the difficult problems of amateur bands is to get the students to practice properly. Many of them leave their instru-

---

Popularity is indeed a curious thing. It is remarkable how soon the so-called "popular" compositions are consigned to oblivion.—*F. Hiller.*

ments in the band room from one rehearsal to another, and if these rehearsals are a week apart, not much good can be accomplished. It is not possible for any person to become proficient on any instrument when he only sees that instrument once a week at rehearsals. No one who plays so little can develop an embouchure, nor can he have a good attack, a good tone, or good intonation. Such players cannot be of any musical value to a band, and should be dropped for the good of the organization. Wind instrument players must practice a certain amount each day in order to have control of their tones. A wind instrument that is only used once a week is never in fit condition to give satisfaction. Band players should also be compelled to take their music with them for home practice and study so that they may become thoroughly familiar with their parts.

There are thousands of amateur bands of all kinds in the country today, but those which rank highest are the ones that devote the most time to rehearsals. It would be a wonderful thing if our young bands could have daily rehearsals.

At all rehearsals the conductor must have full power and authority inasmuch as he is wholly responsible for the proper interpretation and rendition of the music. He should have a definite idea as to the effects, tonal balance, climaxes, and so on, that he wishes to achieve and must plan beforehand the best and most direct method of achieving his end. He must be strict and impartial and overlook no faults, for any defects not corrected at the start will be more difficult to rectify as time goes on. The players must realize that the conductor is prompt and business-like. Rehearsals should start promptly. At the appointed hour the conductor should rap his baton for attention. Not a word should be spoken after that, except by the conductor. The music should be properly distributed by the librarian before the rehearsal starts. Before starting to play the performers should tune their instruments. At no time (rehearsal or concert) should the conductor proceed until the tuning has been attended to. When the conductor signals the band to stop so that he can make his corrections or suggestions, all performers should cease playing immediately. A rehearsal which is not conducted along the lines of strictest discipline is of no avail whatever.

Never judge a composition on a first hearing, for what pleases at first is not always the best, and the works of great masters require study.—*Schumann.*

Most conductors keep their bands playing too steadily at rehearsals, and as a result the lips tire so quickly that after an hour no good is accomplished. The players lose all lip control. It would be advisable after fifty minutes or an hour to make an intermission of ten minutes. This should be done at concerts as well. Most bands are overplayed. Not even professional bands should be allowed to play too steadily, either at rehearsals or concerts.

A serious fault of most band rehearsals is that too many different numbers are played, instead of concentrating on a few. Not enough detailed rehearsing is done. The idea of sectional rehearsals is a most important one. The Clarinets can be rehearsed separately on occasion, then the Saxophones, etc.,—then all the reeds. The Cornets can be rehearsed, the Trombones—then all the brasses. Then when the entire band plays together the results will be much better.

Whether or not anything is accomplished at the rehearsals depends entirely upon the conductor. He is the king. If he has the proper qualifications and the proper system for rehearsing, fine results will soon be apparent. If there are certain players who do not keep pace with the progress of the others he must seek new ones. He must assume full responsibility for the playing of his band. The band which does the most and the best rehearsing should make the most rapid progress.

Books are but waste paper unless we spend in action the wisdom we get from thought.—*Bulwer.*

CHAPTER XII.

PROGRAMS

The making of interesting and well-balanced programs is an art in itself; it is a thing to which the conductor should give much time and careful thought. A poorly constructed program will gain the favor of neither the audience nor the players even though it be well rendered. Great opportunities are lost through programs which are not properly conceived. A program which has plenty of contrast, and which shows the capabilities of the band to the best possible advantage, is the one to be rendered.

A program which is too long is its own worst enemy. It is boring to an audience as well as tiring to the players. An audience should never be placed in the position of wishing that a concert were over. An audience should never be overfed, but on the contrary should be sent away clamoring and wishing for more; that is the best, in fact, the only way of getting them to come back for future programs. Then again, when a program is too long bands cannot do justice to it. The lips of wind instrument players cannot stand the strain beyond a certain point, and when the lips are tired, good results are impossible to attain. Every capable conductor will understand this and will take this fact into consideration at all concerts and rehearsals.

One of the greatest mistakes bandmasters make is their method of giving "encores" or "extra numbers." It has been the custom of most bandmasters for many years to render an "encore" or "extra number" after each number on the program, even though the applause of the audience does not warrant it. As a matter of fact, most bandmasters do not even wait for the applause of the listeners. Immediately upon the termination of the given program number, they take up their "extra" piece, just giving the players time enough to turn the page. This, to my mind, is a very serious mistake. Music should not be hurled or forced upon an audience in such a manner. Such

A man often forgets his friends, his native land, and sometimes his language, but the songs of childhood and youth never fade from the memory.—*Anon.*

tactics tire an audience, and drive them away. Orchestras do *not* do that. If the listeners are sufficiently impressed—if they feel that a band has given an artistic performance, if they have been inspired or uplifted, they will show it by long, loud, and unmistakable applause and enthusiasm. That is the time for an encore. Why force any extra music on an audience? If they want it they will ask for it through their applause, and then there will be a point to it. The old style concert had no high spots because the audience never got the chance to express itself properly. When an extra is demanded, the players themselves get a real thrill, and the feeling that their efforts are being appreciated. They are inspired to play with still more enthusiasm. It is not to be expected that an audience will respond to each program piece with great enthusiasm, for some types of music do not inspire such expression of emotion. A program which is properly built, however, will contain some numbers which will, if properly rendered, make the audience react. The conductor will generally have a pretty good notion in advance of what these compositions will be.

After a long Overture or other important piece, the band is entitled to at least two or three minutes rest in order to be fit to do justice to the next number. It has been my observation that most bands are completely "played-out" when intermission time comes. The second part of the program always suffers as a consequence. A good rule to follow is to play "extras" only when they are actually demanded by the audience. The difference between the words "encore" and "extra" is not generally understood. "Encore" means "again," "recall" or "repetition," and should in reality only apply when the piece is repeated. Bands seldom give "encores" in the true sense of the world. They generally render "extras".

A concert program should under no circumstances last longer than two hours and even that is too long. An hour and a half to an hour and three-quarters is the ideal time, and even then there should be an intermission of about ten minutes, and a little breathing spell between the program numbers. A plan of this kind will give the players a chance to give the best that is in them throughout the concert. This is a matter to which conductors must give a thought. It is not a question of seeing how much can be given within a certain time, but rather how fine a performance. Long programs, without sufficient breath-

Is there a heart that music cannot melt?—*Beattie.*

ing spaces have the same effect as the steady grinding of a hand organ.

How should a program be built? And what points must the conductor take into consideration? Compositions should be selected which offer a variety of contrast and moods. It is not generally wise, for instance, to play two very slow pieces in succession, or two that are precisely the same in character. There are occasions, in certain types of programs, and for certain audiences, when this can be done successfully, but not as a general thing. My suggestions in regard to the program are intended for the average mixed audience. It is not always good policy to play two extremely long works in succession. Many of the so-called Operatic Fantasies (or Selections), and Comic Opera Selections are too long. They can generally be cut so that the more important and pleasing parts are retained. This seems to be an age of speed. Audiences do not wish to sit through long-drawn-out works unless they are particularly effective and interesting.

It is not my intention to try to set up a definite style of program, but each conductor must consider his audience as well as his players. He either wants to entertain or educate his audience, or both. Two or three numbers of the same type should not follow each other. If they do, the audience loses interest, and when that happens, the band and its conductor are not successful. The conductor must be a sort of student of psychology. He must study how best to win his audiences and keep them interested. Fine performances are, of course, the first requisite.

As a rule, I like to start a band concert with a Grand March, for this gives the players a chance to "warm up" and get their lips in good trim—a great necessity. It is rather trying to start a concert with something that is very delicate in structure, before the players have had an opportunity of preparing. After a brilliant opening number, they are in a better condition for the performance of anything that is delicate. The conductor should be sure that he has the best available arrangement of each number he programs.

Another important item that conductors must take into consideration when preparing their programs, is whether they will have the time necessary to rehearse all the pieces properly.

Every difficulty slurred over will be a ghost to disturb your repose later on.
—*Chopin.*

Nothing should ever be performed in public that has not been properly rehearsed. The conductor should never take a chance with any music, however simple, which has not been properly prepared. His reputation is at stake, and as a leader he must assume the responsibility for anything he conducts.

As extra numbers Marches are always appropriate, but it is not wise to perform too many of them at any single concert, for they are tiring to the lips of the players. Marches that are played should be rehearsed as carefully as any other compositions. "Extra" numbers should never be long.

Much more could be said about the preparation of programs inasmuch as it is one of the most important items which the conductor has to consider. It does not suffice to select a lot of compositions at random, and place them in any rotation, just to fill the required time at a concert. Proper program building requires thought and careful study. Consideration must be given from the standpoint of the conductor, the players and the audience. There should be some reason for the placing of each composition at a certain place on the program—some thought behind it.

Many bandmasters make the very serious mistake of playing compositions that are beyond the capabilities of their players. It would seem that the bandmaster who indulges in this is not capable, for it hardly seems possible that he would be willing to allow his band to perform a work in public if he realized that it was being poorly played. It is much more creditable to play a simple piece well than a difficult one poorly. The conductor who takes chances in public is a detriment to his organization. The catalogs of the various publishers contain new band editions of great value, and most of them specify the degree of simplicity or difficulty of their publications. Each concert program that is offered should represent the very best effort of the conductor and the performers.

Many of the bands now are taking pattern after the symphony orchestras and including descriptive or explanatory notes on the important music rendered. This is to be encouraged as it helps the listeners to a greater enjoyment of the music. These explanations need not be too technical, nor should they be unintelligible and uninteresting even to musicians and

---

It is in music, perhaps, that the soul most nearly attains the great end for which, when inspired by the poetic sentiment, it struggles—the creation of supernal beauty.
—*Edgar Allan Poe.*

music lovers, as explanatory notes on the symphony concert programs often are. Anything that can be done to help the audience to a better understanding, and keener enjoyment of the music should be done. A little idea of what the music is intended to convey, or a few facts about the composer, will add materially to the interest of the listeners.

To make a home out of a household, given the raw materials—to wit: a wife, children, a friend or two, and a house—two other things are necessary. These are a good fire and good music. And inasmuch as we can do without the fire for half the year, I may say music is the one essential.—*R. L. Stevenson.*

CHAPTER XIII.

THE LIBRARY

To acquire the proper kind of a library should be the aim of every Band. This is not, however, a very simple matter. The Orchestra is not confronted with any difficulty in this regard for the reason that it is standardized in all parts of the world. Bands have a different instrumentation in nearly every country and therefore most of the publications of France and Italy, for example, are not satisfactory for our American Bands.

There are other difficulties too. Most of the published band music consists of arrangements or transcriptions of the music of the masters or other standard music which was originally composed for orchestra. Some of these arrangements are excellently done, others in a very mediocre manner, and many of them are so badly arranged that even a fine band cannot make them sound acceptable. Much of the music that was arranged and published in the past is scarcely worth the paper on which it is printed, and as standards have changed, many things that were accepted forty or fifty years ago could not and should not be tolerated today. Old band music was to a large extent poorly arranged, and in a strictly commercial manner. Not much thought was given to tonal coloring, tonal balance, phrasing, etc., In hundreds of instances, the editions looked as if they had never been proof-read. But in those days bands could secure nothing else, and their performances suffered as a consequence. As time went on, some of the publishers endeavored to improve these old editions by having them corrected and by having missing parts added to the instrumentation. Even this did not make good arrangements of them. Bands were not very seriously considered. Many people were prejudiced against them. Finally, a new era in bands and band music arose due to the efforts of some few bandmasters of prominence as well as to the introduction of bands in most of

---

In music you will soon find out what personal benefit there is in being serviceable.
—*Ruskin.*

our schools, high schools, colleges, and institutions of all kinds.
The interest in band music began to increase, creating a demand
for better band music.

The average bandmaster, however, is still completely at
sea when it comes to selecting music for his library, and there
is ample reason for this. When it is apparent, for instance, that
almost any well known composition can be had in from one to
ten different editions and totally different arrangements, one
can readily understand with what a difficult task the conductor is confronted. As an example, take Wagner's Tannhäuser
Overture. It can be purchased in several different English
band arrangements; four or five different German editions,
and in a number of American arrangements. It must be remembered that each one of these arrangements is totally different, having been prepared by different men, and some of them
even done in different keys. Some of these arrangements are
simplified. Some are cheaper than others. Some are advertised as giving equally good results when played with twenty
or a hundred players (an impossibility) and so on.

My library is large, and contains certain compositions in
as many as five or six different arrangements and editions. I
have gathered all these arrangements in order to select the
best for performance at my concerts. In some instances none
of these arrangements are strictly satisfactory from an artistic
standpoint. Bandmasters cannot be expected to buy several
editions of each piece they want. What are they to do?

It is the duty of bandmasters to study the various catalogs
before purchasing, and not accept any edition that is sent them,
because they happen to deal with a certain firm. It is possible
in many instances to have music sent on approval for trial. This
would give an opportunity to hear and learn the differences
of the various arrangements. Of course, the capable conductor
should be able to judge of the merits of the different editions,
especially if he is at all familiar with the work in its original
form. Inquiry should be made as to the different editions, and
advice sought as to the best. The best arrangement is generally
the easiest, and of course always sounds best. It may not be
the cheapest.

I have conducted bands in all parts of the United States
and Canada, both amateur and professional. I have found
very often that where there are three, four, or more arrange-

---

Popular music, after all, is only familiar music.—*Theodore Thomas.*

ments of a certain composition I am to conduct, the band will
have the very worst published edition. What does that mean?
Simply that the band possesses a library of very old and poor
arrangements, or else that the conductor has not taken the
time or the pains to get the best. This is an injustice to the
players, as well as to the listeners. The inferior arrangement
is generally more difficult, colorless, and lacking in all the essentials of the original score. It is also faulty in most other
respects. Some arrangements are made so badly that the cornet is playing what the flute or clarinets should be doing, or
the trombone is playing what another instrument should have,
etc. Then again, many of these arrangers, in assigning a tenor
vocal (operatic) aria, will give it to some instrument in the
baritone range. This is a very frequent fault. Another serious
fault is to choose bad keys, for no good reason. In general,
band editions have not always been what they should be.

Another one of the most tragic drawbacks to the progress
of bands and band music is the fact that most of the older editions did not have a suitable part from which the conductor
could direct. Various band parts including Eb Cornet, or 1st or
Solo Bb Cornet have been labeled "Conductor" in the past,
and whether it was a classical overture or an operatic fantasie
that was all the conductor had to guide him. Frequently a number of bars of rest would occur, and in such places not even
"cued in" notes were printed. Imagine a conductor trying to
give a first-class performance under such circumstances. No
wonder that for a long time bands were pursuing the down-
ward path. There is no place today for the conductor who is
willing to tolerate such conditions.

Conductors who do not exercise care in the choice of their
music are not doing their duty and, therefore, much that has
retarded the progress of the band is due to them.

Fortunately, our prominent American publishers are now
issuing editions that are a credit to them as well as to the cause
of band music. They realize that we are living in different
times and that the standard must be raised. Most of our publishers are members of the American Bandmasters' Association,
and have taken an active part in its program for raising the
standard of bands and band music. During the past few years

If young men had music and pictures to interest them, to engage them, and
satisfy many of their impulses and to enliven their days, they would not go to the
low pleasures of the streets; they would have an alternative and would be too fas-
tidious to do so.—*Bernard Shaw.*

they have done everything in their power to promote the cause of better editions. The arrangements are better. They are more carefully edited in regard to phrasing, dynamics, etc., and in most instances no more double parts are printed. Second and third Clarinets—second and third Cornets—first and second Trombones, etc.—instead of being printed in double notes on one sheet are issued separately. Then all new standard music has a conductor's part of three, four, or five staves, so that the conductor can have a concrete idea of what the various instruments have to play. This is a sort of condensed score. Some firms have even issued complete band scores, but these have not become popular as yet, because of the cost, because of the fact that most bandmasters have not become familiar with score-reading, and because many band concerts are given in the open—where it is almost impossible to cope with the constant turning of pages, especially if there is a little wind.

But even with these new and better editions, it still remains necessary for conductors to ascertain which is the best arrangement procurable. If there are four arrangements of a certain composition obtainable, one of them must be the best. That is the one to secure. Good arrangements will make bands sound one hundred percent better. Conductors should leave no stone unturned in their endeavor to secure the best.

Another very serious fault of conductors is that most of them secure music that is far beyond the capabilities of their players. Much more credit would be reflected upon the band if compositions were chosen which the players could perform creditably. The simplest music is difficult to perform well. A church hymn well played is worth a thousand times more than an overture poorly executed. By performing music that is too difficult, the progress of an organization is being materially retarded. No audience cares whether a composition is simple or difficult, but they want it well played.

Most bands are called upon to play patriotic music. This is one of their functions. There are hundreds of arrangements of "The Star Spangled Banner", "America", "Dixie", etc. No two of them are alike, and no two of them seem to agree either in ryhthm or melodic progression; most of them are old and worse than atrocious. Publishers will soon issue first class arrangements of all the patriotic songs and folk melodies. Bands have a habit, however, of playing these songs without music,

I verily think, and I am not ashamed to say, that, next to Divinity, no art is comparable to music.—*Martin Luther.*

"vamping" or "faking" them. This is one of the great band evils. Its results are that no two performers play the melody alike, that the correct harmony is totally lacking, and that even the trombones and basses generally consider it a good opportunity to play the melody part. People listening to such a performance generally form a lastingly unfavorable impression of bands and band music. The conductor who permits this "faking" or "vamping" of "The Star Spangled Banner" or any other music should not be tolerated, for he is working against the interest of bands. And then again, how often is one privileged to hear a stirring or inspiring performance of the national anthem? How many bands have ever actually taken the pains to rehearse this music? There is just as much to rehearse in music of this type as in any other form of music.

Good arrangements, good music and fine editions are just as important as good instruments. What good is one without the other ? Each band should have a music or library fund to make it possible to secure music as the need arises. Bands that persist in using some of the faulty editions of the past should discard them and replenish their shelves. Money spent in the proper type of music is a fine investment, the most important to any band. Never seek the cheapest arrangement. It may be good, but on the other hand, it may be the worst. The best is always the cheapest in the end. The conductor who is not sure which arrangement to secure should make every possible effort to find out.

Naturally, every band must have a Librarian whose duty it is to look after the music and see that it is properly catalogued. He must repair any torn parts and report any member who mutilates his part. Each part should be cared for as though it were a valuable book. The music should be catalogued in a book or card system, or both.

As stated before, most music that is rendered by bands was originally written for orchestra. The great composers conceived most of their works for orchestra. Many of our present day composers, however, have through the influence of the American Bandmasters' Association been induced to write for band. The band will reach greater heights when more original music is written for it. The composers of the future will most assuredly produce more works for band, and in order to encourage them, the bandmasters must produce as many of these original band compositions as possible. In this manner the band will soon secure a library and repertoire of its own.

THE GOLDMAN BAND
(Showing seating arrangement and properly built stage.)

CHAPTER XIV.

SEATING ARRANGEMENT

Much of the success of the playing of the band, at least in regard to tonal balance, depends upon the manner in which the various sections are placed. Until a few years ago the seating of a band was done in the same old stereotyped way; the clarinets and other reeds to the left of the conductor, and the cornets and other brasses immediately to his right. In those days, the conductors probably felt that it was necessary to have two of their most important players—the first clarinetist and first cornetist near at hand.

Fifteen or more years ago I experimented for many weeks during my season of summer concerts on the Green at Columbia University. I felt that better tonal balance and effects could be achieved through an improved seating arrangement. I put my ideas into effect, and placed the first clarinets to my left and the second and third clarinets immediately to my right. In other words, I placed my reeds and wood-winds to my right and left, and also immediately in front of me. This gave more of an orchestral effect since the reeds really represent the strings. The players at first resented this change, claiming that the old seating arrangement had been good enough for years. There was a great deal of criticism of the new plan, but finally those who objected most strenuously admitted that it was a change for the better, and a great step forward. The season after the plan was put into effect, more experiments were conducted at the Mall in Central Park and further changes found advisable.

After the second series of experiments, practically every one agreed that the old seating arrangements had outlived their usefulness. Despite that fact, however, there are still bands that cling to the old system, feeling that because a thing was done a certain way fifty years ago it should still be done so. The Goldman Band was probably the first organization to experiment with seating, and finally to adopt the improved

Music is a stimulant to mental exertion.—*D'Israeli.*

system. In the early broadcasting days many experiments were made, and finally even the broadcasting companies insisted upon the bands being seated according to the "Goldman plan" (as they called it) to secure the best results.

The old style of having the brasses at the immediate right of the conductor made it almost impossible to secure and maintain a proper balance. In fortissimo passages the reeds and woodwinds were completely overpowered. By surrounding the conductor with reeds and having all brasses at a distance it is far more easy to secure a good tonal balance as well as good tonal quality and attack. The conductor has far better control at all times and he secures a quicker and better response. These directors who still cling to the old system are the losers by it, and are doing their organizations a great injustice.

A definite and set rule cannot be made for the seating of bands in general, because everything depends upon the acoustics of the place where the concert is given. However, it is always wise to group the reeds and woodwinds to the right, left and front of the conductor. Each band should have some sort of prescribed seating plan and the librarian should arrange this set-up wherever the band plays. After a rehearsal of a few moments, the conductor should be able to judge whether any of the instruments should be placed differently.

The picture in connection with this chapter gives the seating arrangement of the Goldman Band which has been found very satisfactory. I was not able to place all of my players as I wished because of the narrowness of the bandstand at the rear.

Here are some very important items to be considered. The proper placing of the brasses is far more difficult than that of the reeds and woodwinds. The reason will probably seem strange and new to most people. The tone of the reed instruments is emitted through the finger holes and not through the bell or end of the instrument. The tone of brass instruments is emitted through the bell and goes in the direction to which the instrument is pointed. Now these are very important items, far more important than most bandmasters and even symphony conductors imagine.

It would make little or no difference whether the clarinetist —for instance—faced to the right or to the left, or whether he turned his back to the conductor, because the tones come

Without enthusiasm one will never accomplish anything in art.—*Schumann.*

through the finger holes. This is another important reason for placing all reeds and woods around the conductor. It matters not whether their instruments are pointed North, South, East, or West. With the brasses, however, it is a totally different matter. It is my strong conviction that all brass instruments should be of the "bell front" model—that is, they should be built so that the bell or end of the instrument points to the front. Trumpets, Cornets and Trombones are, of course, built that way. All other brass instruments, with the exception of the French Horn, should be "bell-front." To explain this more fully, it must be remembered that Baritones, Euphoniums, Tenor Horns, and Tubas are most generally built in what is known as "Upright Models" with the bells pointing upwards. It has occurred frequently that in one band there were as many as four differently constructed Tubas. There was one upright model pointing up over the player's left shoulder, another upright model pointing over the next player's right shoulder, and still another with a bell-front, etc. What was the result of this? Simply that each of these players was sending his tones in a totally different direction and they could not be properly merged in the whole. I also experimented in this matter, and was soon convinced that "Bell-front" brasses are a necessity. Furthermore, I have noticed that the Trombone players often sit so that their instruments point to the East—while the Cornetists and Trumpeters are pointing their instruments to the West, North, or South. This is also bad. It frequently happens that all the instruments of one choir, all of the Cornets or all of the Trombones are not pointed in the same direction.

I contend, after many experiments, that not alone should all brass instruments (French Horns excepted) be of the "bell-front" model, but, also that the players be seated so that the bells be pointed directly toward the audience, or very nearly so. This will blend the tones of the noble brasses as no other arrangement will, and an absolutely stirring and inspiring organ effect will be obtained.

I was, for ten years, a trumpet player in the Metropolitan Opera House Orchestra, and was at one time employed as an expert by a large band instrument house in New York. In the testing of brass instruments, I soon learned that to test an instrument properly I would have to stand in the same position and play in the same direction, that is, toward the same wall.

Song brings of itself a cheerfulness that wakes the heart to joy.—*Euripides.*

If I played the same tones, the same theme, and faced the side or rear wall which might be nearer or further away, the effect would be totally different. All competent brass players realize this fact. The nearness or distance of a wall, or whether one plays toward a window, a metal door, or heavy hangings, affects not only the tonal quality, but the blowing quality of the brasses. Therefore, all brasses must point their bells in the one direction. A short experiment will prove this.

No Symphony Orchestra is getting the proper results from its brasses today, for, in most instances, if the Trumpets are pointed toward the audience, the Trombones are probably sending their tones across the stage to one of the side walls, and the Tuba may be sending its tones up in the air, where they do not blend as they should, or where they are half lost. If symphony conductors would experiment with this and play a Choral, with a pianissimo, and then a crescendo to a fortissimo climax, they would get a great thrill. Brasses must and will soon be properly placed.

The greatest difficulty in band seating is the placement of the French Horns because they are the most delicate of the brasses and also because their bells are held close to the players' laps. Conductors must experiment with the placing of these important instruments for what may be good in one hall will not be satisfactory in another. And then again special consideration must be given to them for open-air performances. Of course, placing the players on platforms helps. As a matter of fact, each row of players in a band should be raised higher than those in front. In other words there should be three or four levels. This offers many advantages to conductor and players. It makes it possible for the conductor to get an unobstructed view of each of the players, and enables them to get a clear view of him, both of which results are necessary. Then, it enables the tones of the brass instruments to ring out in all their beauty and brilliancy, whereas if the band were seated on a level floor, each brass player would be playing into the clothes of the person in front of him, thus muffling the tones.

The raised platform levels also make a finer stage picture for the audience, and permits them to see the various instruments in action whereas a band on a level floor can never be seen except by those sitting in the balconies. A band of one hundred on a level floor will look like twenty-five or thirty.

Learn all there is to learn, and then choose your own path.—*Handel.*

For tonal effects, and for precision, the raised platform levels are necessary. The conductor should have a platform high enough to give him a perfect view of those playing under him, and large enough to enable him to move with freedom.

The problem of open-air playing must be carefully studied. Those who have the proper type of bandstand, in which the acoustics are good, are fortunate indeed. The "shell" bandstand is the most satisfactory.

The proper placing of the Percussion Section of the Band is frequently a very puzzling problem. When the drums are placed in the rear against a wall, especially when there is a sounding board or shell, they generally sound too loud. In fact, as a general thing in most bands the drums are always too loud, so much so that when a real fortissimo or a huge climax is desired they are totally ineffective.

While on the subject of proper seating, it might be well to stress the importance of a well-arranged stage. Chairs should be well placed, and alike. Music stands should be of one kind and the players should be dressed alike. Where two men sit at the same stand, the second—or inside man— is always required to turn the pages of the music, and, in the open, he is the one to pin the clamps on in case of wind.

Proper seating is a thing of such vast importance—that no conductor should be satisfied unless he feels that he is securing the best possible tonal effects and tonal blending.

If you love music, hear it; go to operas, concerts, and pay fiddlers to play for you.
—*Earl of Chesterfield.*

CHAPTER XV.

INTONATION

In a good band the tuning should be very accurate, in fact just as good as that of a first class orchestra. A fine band frequently tunes better than an orchestra. It has often been noticed in orchestras that the wind section is much flatter than the string section. The strings are frequently unwilling to tune down.

It is, of course, necessary that each player tune his instruments properly before the start of a rehearsal or concert. Brass instruments are tuned by moving the slides in or out. When sharp, the slides, or a particular slide, are drawn as may be required, and when flat, the necessary slides are pushed in according to the need. Reed players have not as much leeway in the matter of tuning. They can, however, adjust the mouthpiece or the sections of their instruments in some instances. Many players believe that when this is done before a concert, they cannot possibly play out of tune. The adjusting of the slides, and so forth, is just the preliminary step. If the player does not possess control and a very keen ear he cannot possibly play in tune under any circumstances. The ear and lips work simultaneously. Players who do not devote daily practice to the proper kind of exercises will never have control of their tones, nor will they be able to play in tune, even though they have good ears. Conductors should help the ear-training of their players, by making them decide whether they are out of tune or not, and whether too sharp or flat. All players should be able to decide that for themselves. If they can't, it stands to reason that their ears are not sensitive enough to discern. In such instances special attention should be given to their ear training, and if after a sufficient time they make no progress, they should be dropped from the membership, if the band is to

When gripping Grief the Heart doth wound,
And doleful Dumps the Mind oppress,
Then music, with her silver sound,
With speedy help doth lend redress.
—*Shakespeare.*

make progress. Young players must be taught to listen carefully to each and every note that they play. No wind instrument that was ever made is absolutely in tune, but any one can be played in tune, if the player has a good embouchure and a good ear. He must learn to adjust or favor certain notes on his instrument or "humor" them. Whether in solo or ensemble playing the performer must be able to adjust his tones.

It has been known that two fine players could use the same cornet, for instance, and one would find a certain note sharp, and the other find the same note flat. Yet they could both play the note perfectly in tune, because they both had a properly developed embouchure, and a well-trained ear. A person might purchase a Stradivarius violin, and not secure a fine tonal quality, or play in tune. He would have to have the proper finger and bow facility together with a very accurate ear. A bad instrument in the hands of a good player therefore generally sounds better than a fine instrument in the hands of a poor player.

Heat and cold affect the intonation of all wind instruments. Heat sharpens, while cold flattens them. If instruments are cold they are easily warmed up by playing for a few minutes, or blowing the warm breath through them without making any sounds. It is frequently necessary to adjust the slides again after having played a little while. The ear must always be alert to deficiencies. Damp weather and moisture do not have any effect on the intonation, although they affect the mechanism of wood instruments. It has been found that the brass instruments sound even more brilliant when the atmosphere is moist, and they seem to blow and respond more freely.

When brass instruments are played with mutes they are frequently thrown out of tune. In most instances they become sharp.

Good intonation is one of the prime requisites of a good band and it is that to which the conductor should give much time and attention. He must make it his business to find out if any of his players are incapable of knowing when they are not playing in tune. Good intonation and good tonal quality go hand in hand. The pitch is generally taken from the Oboe. In orchestras the note A is used for tuning purposes, but in bands Bb is used. This would be the open C on all Bb instruments. The note A could be used just as well for bands, for

---

Only he can benefit from praise who can appreciate criticism.—*Schumann.*

after all, the tuning note is just for the general pitch. Sounding any one note does not, of course, tune the entire instrument.

The study of solfege (or solmisation) is highly to be recommended for the development of an accurate musical ear. Certainly, the training of no musician can be called complete unless he is able to recognize intervals, and to judge them accurately. To this end, solfege training should occupy a small amount of the rehearsal time of any amateur band. The results will be immediately apparent in the band's performance.

Of all liberal arts music has the greatest influence over the passions, and it is that to which the legislator ought to give his greatest encouragement.—*Napoleon I.*

CHAPTER XVI.

SIGHT READING

Although no special rules can be made for the study and improvement of sight reading, there is much advice and useful information which will be of great value and assistance to the many students who are anxious to make progress in this particular branch of musical training. There are many professionals and amateurs who play very well, but who read music with much difficulty. It is a well-known fact also that many good soloists are very poor sight readers, but this is readily explained. A man who devotes all his time and energy to solo playing, perfects himself in a certain repertoire. This repertoire may consist of any number of solos. He studies the numbers at his leisure, and devotes as much time as he sees fit to each solo. He practices until his aim is accomplished.

With the orchestra and band player of today it is quite a different matter. He cannot really be successful unless he is a good reader. Most professional bands do comparatively little rehearsing and it is always probable that some occasions will arise when a number will have to be performed without having been rehearsed, through lack of time or for other reasons. Then again in first-class organizations the leader expects his men to be good readers, and to be able to do justice to any new music he may put before them. Good bands composed of proficient players generally have little time to waste.

In order to become a proficient reader, it is necessary above everything else to have a good idea of one's instrument, and to be able to play at least fairly well. Naturally, if one is not master of the technic of an exercise or piece, he certainly cannot play it at sight. *Therefore it is essential that the student should not attempt to read at sight anything that is technically beyond his capabilities as a player.* The best and most systematic way of improvement is to practice reading from the start. For example, if one is a beginner and playing simple exercises, he should try

---

All one's life is music, if one touches the notes rightly, and in time.—*Ruskin.*

to read exercises of a similar nature, in another book, if possible. He should endeavor to play the exercise without hesitation. Even if he makes a mistake or plays a false note he should continue playing and keep the time and rhythm intact. At the second reading he may corrrect his mistakes.

It is imperative that the student have a good idea of the rudiments of music, or he never can become a good sight reader. He must be familiar with the various keys and signatures, and must know the value of notes and rests, and above all, must play strictly in time. In sight reading it is necessary to look ahead constantly. While playing one note, the next one must be anticipated and the time and value of each note remembered. This requires a quick eye and some brain work, but the first requisite is a general and positive knowledge of all notes and their time values, and a thorough familiarity with all fingerings. If a person has mastered all this, he should have little or no difficulty in becoming a good sight reader. As stated before, there are no set rules, and one does not need a teacher. Sight reading is simply a matter of practice and experience, and should begin with simple exercises; progress is made by degrees. After a little practice one will be able to read an entire bar ahead, and consequently keep the music going without hesitation. The principal thing is to be able to look ahead and keep the eyes and ears on the alert.

There is nothing more useful to a musician than being able to read well. He can then familiarize himself with all kinds of music, and derive unlimited pleasure from his accomplishment. He can read new music as another person would read a book, and even if he does not play it as well as it should be played, he has a comprehensive idea of what it is, and can master it perfectly with practice. After one becomes a ready reader, the eye and the ear have become so well trained that the player can look at a piece of music and know just how it sounds, without playing a note.

Almost anyone can become a good sight reader with a little patience and practice. It is the duty of every teacher to give his pupils exercises in sight reading, but the student himself can do more than any teacher, by devoting a little time each day to playing something that is not familiar to him. Playing over what has been played before is not sight reading.

Keep time. How sour sweet music is, when time is broke, and no proportion kept.—*Shakespeare.*

Bandmasters should train their bands in the art of sight-reading. This can be done in a very simple and systematic manner. It is a good idea to start the "ensemble sight-reading" in young bands as soon as they begin to perform pieces. A large number of simple exercises and pieces are available for this purpose. As the players improve in their playing, more advanced music may be attempted. All amateur bands should have the benefit of this fine type of training, and even professional bands should read over new music as frequently as possible. Sight-reading should be a regular part of the schedule of every band. The band which is capable of doing good sight-reading can generally be depended upon to respond readily to every signal and every wish of the conductor. The good sight reader generally plays more accurately than the other players, and he gets more joy from his playing than others do. Sight reading makes the players more keen, more alert, more responsive and more dependable.

Professional players who have played in a theatre, where a production has had a run of a year or more, for instance, will tell you that they lose their sightreading ability unless they practice reading new and unfamiliar music steadily. Musicians who have toured with bands for very long seasons where only two or three programs were necessary because of the constant traveling will admit that if they had not continued to read new music in their leisure they too would have lost their sight-reading ability.

In the various band contests held throughout the country, sight-reading is one of the important items. This is a good idea. Many of the bands spend all their rehearsal time on the actual contest pieces. If six or eight months are spent in this manner, naturally sight-reading is compelled to suffer.

One additional suggestion for the improvement of sight-reading is this:—Perform the music very slowly at first, in order to play the right notes at least, and to give them their designated values, at the same time observing which notes are slurred, and which detached. The proper observance of the rests is as important as that of the notes. To become a good sight-reader all performers should at first play their music *slowly enough to allow them to perform it correctly*—observing all dynamic markings, etc. The idea is to play it *correctly at*

Music is fundamental—one of the great sources of life, health, strength and happiness.—*Luther Burbank.*

sight. As a matter of fact, it is generally a good idea to practice all rapid music in a slower tempo at first to insure correctness and precision. If this is achieved from the start, the proper tempo can soon be realized through practice. The best sight readers are those who at first have the patience to read their music slowly and correctly.

"God sent his singers upon the earth
With songs of sadness and of mirth,
That they might touch the hearts of men
And bring them back to heaven again."
—*Longfellow.*

CHAPTER XVII.

POINTERS IN PHRASING

Phrasing is the art of dividing musical sentences into rhythmical sections; this being effected by breathing points, various articulations, slurs and accents. It is much the same as punctuation in writing. According to the dictionary, phrasing means: Firstly, the bringing out into proper relief of the phrases (whether motives, figures, subjects, or passages), as regards their individual melodic and rhythmic characterization and their relative importance; secondly, the signs of notation devised to further the above end.

If we were to write a letter and omit the punctuation marks, such as commas, periods, question marks, etc., it would have no sense. If we were to try to read a book which was not punctuated, we would soon learn that there was no meaning in it, and would be compelled to give up in disgust. In music, phrasing takes the place of punctuation, and, therefore, any rendition that is not properly phrased, is devoid of all value and understanding. The mere playing of a mass of notes does not constitute music. In order to interpret intelligently, music must be divided into sections or phrases, first of all—and then the proper expressions and tonal color given to each passage, by strictly observing every graduation of sound, and other marks indicated by the composer.

The player will probably now ask: "But how are we to see these invisible commas, dashes, periods, etc., in music, so as to be able to keep from giving faulty and monotonous renditions?" First of all, the eye and the intelligence are of vast importance in this task, but it is more easily solved by the ear. Before one's phrasing can be properly corrected, the development of a sense of time and rhythm must be complete. Instrumental music is considered more difficult to phrase well than vocal music, because in the latter one can be guided by the words

---

Music is one of the most forcible instruments for training, for arousing, for governing the mind and spirit of man.—*Gladstone.*

to a great extent. In instrumental music, we must rely upon the ear and our good taste. In the playing of wind instruments the performer must endeavor to imitate singing. A song or aria, for instance, should be played as an artist would sing it. The reading or memorizing of the words will help to a considerable extent towards good phrasing. When a new piece is being studied, the player should look it over carefully and decide when and where breath should be taken. Most players indulge in the very faulty habit of playing as much as they can on one breath; then they can not catch a new breath quickly enough. The tones and the articulation are always bound to suffer if one does not possess perfect breath-control at all times. Breathing in the proper places saves one's energy, and gives perfect ease, comfort and control. The end of a piece should find one as fresh as in the beginning, if the breathing is properly conducted.

To learn the art of phrasing properly, one should start with the very simplest kind of songs. Melodies with which one is familiar and which contain even and well-defined phrases should be taken up first. There are many little songs in which the phrases are very evenly divided; that is, where one phrase is just as long as another, and often contains the same number of notes. But other songs are again very irregular in form, and the proper phrasing becomes more intricate. We may hear two artists render a song, and each may phrase it in a slightly different manner, and still both interpretations may be highly artistic. Steadfast rules cannot be made.

The beginner, who, as a rule, is satisfied with being able to emit the proper sounds, should be taught correct phrasing from the very outset, so that when he is advanced, his interpretations will be musically interesting and sound. If this important item is cultivated systematically, from the beginning, the student will become so proficient that he can see at a glance where a phrase starts and where it ends, when and where breath should be taken, etc., and will observe the marks of expression at sight. The player who is simply able to play a mass of notes without regard to form or rhythm is, in most instances, simply the victim of poor teaching, or no teaching at all.

From my own personal experience as a former teacher, I can speak with considerable authority on the subject. The

---

The fine art which, more than any other, ministers to human welfare. Where there is beautiful music it is difficult for discontent to live.—*Herbert Spencer.*

performer who studies alone, is, as a rule, glad if he can produce the notes that are written. The player who has had inferior instruction is but little better off. Many find it so difficult to produce the proper tones and are so glad if they can emit them at all, that nothing further seems to enter their minds. Many a new scholar has played for me, and after listening to him for a few moments I have remarked: "Your phrasing is not very good," whereupon he would answer "What do you mean?" When told that he broke up and distorted the phrases by taking breath in the wrong places, etc., he would be amazed. After remarking the places where he should take breath, he would say: "Why I can play five times as much as that on one breath." That is just where the trouble comes in. Most wind instrument players play as much on one breath as they possibly can, or, in other words, until they are thoroughly exhausted. They do not realize that sometimes a phrase may consist of only a few notes, and these few notes should be separated from the others. Phrases differ in size, and, while some may be quite short, others may be much longer. If we know how to divide the phrases, we will soon learn to take breath according to the length of phrases to be played. In this way we gain perfect control of the tones, can play with the greatest possible ease, and can get to the end of a composition without being fatigued.

If we listen to an artist, whether it be a vocalist or instrumentalist, even though we may know nothing about phrasing, we will realize that there is something noble, interesting and appealing about the performance. We may say to ourselves "Oh! That was wonderful!" but we seldom stop to ascertain why. What makes such a rendition wonderful is that everything is clear-cut and polished. There are no rough edges. The small details have all been mastered. After all, it is the little things that count. Anyone can correct a big mistake, whether he be a musician or not. Almost anyone can detect a false note. An uncultivated ear will know when a tone is scratchy or not clear. Richard Wagner once said: "Look after the small things in music, the large ones will take care of themselves." This is very true. Every good performance depends upon the little details, and how they are worked out.

The player who will devote a little time and attention to learning to phrase properly, will be well rewarded in the end,

---

Language is not subtle enough, tender enough to express all we feel, and when language fails, the highest and deepest longings are translated into music.
—*Ingersoll.*

because first of all, his playing will improve a thousand fold
and he will derive more pleasure from his efforts and have a
better standing as a musician, and lastly, he will play with
less exertion.

Music stands nearest to divinity. I would not give the little I know for all the
treasures of the world.—*Luther.*

CHAPTER XVIII.

SLOW OR SUSTAINED MOVEMENTS

Bands have always shown their greatest and most flagrant weakness in the playing of slow or sustained passages—movements that are marked Andante, Largo, Larghetto, etc.

My experience has proved that the prime test for any band is the playing of a slow movement. At many contests and music festivals which I have attended, one band after another would appear and open its program with a March, then an Overture or other standard or classic work. In the playing of the Marches, it is more difficult to judge the actual quality of a band because of the spirited tempo, and because so many of the inner parts are generally concealed, often covered up by the drums. The overture may start with lively tempo, but as soon as the slow tempo is reached, the bottom seems to fall out of the band, and it is then that one discovers the real weaknesses—the poor tonal quality and the very bad intonation. It is in these slow movements that one can readily see whether the individual players actually have the command and control of an instrument. Good tone and good intonation are the prime assets of fine wind instrument playing. Good phrasing is another of these highly important assets.

The great fault with most wind instrument players is that they do not study long enough or seriously enough, nor do they practice regularly and systematically the necessary exercises each day. One learns the fingering of any brass instrument without any difficulty. Any child can learn that very quickly. The Trombone with its slide positions is somewhat more difficult; also the Reed and Wood instruments; but the difficulty is not insurmountable. In the case of the brass instruments the fingering is easily learned and can be mastered in practically no time, so that when the performer can play the scale and "toot" out some simple tune, however badly, he believes he

Show me the home wherein music dwells, and I shall show you a happy, peaceful and contented home.—*Longfellow*.

82

does not require additional instruction. He never develops a good "embouchure" or any real control of his tone. Under such circumstances, not much can be expected of any player.

It takes more time and practice to develop a good tone and style than it does to master the purely mechanical or technical part of the playing. One can learn to make sounds on any wind instrument in a short time, but what will the quality of these sounds be? In order to play a slow movement or a slow melody acceptably, the performer must have control of his tones; his lips must be properly developed; he must have endurance. In other words, he must have what is known among wind instrument players as an "embouchure." He must also have breath control.

No player can acquire an "embouchure" without daily practice of the proper type of exercises, and unless all the players have control of their lips and of their tones it is impossible for any band to give a good account of itself—particularly in a slow movement. It requires far more lip development and control to render a slow melody artistically than it does to perform fast passages. Players who lack this development and control cannot possibly produce a good quality of tone; neither can they play in tune, or have the necessary endurance.

Now then, how is it possible to acquire these very essential qualities? First of all, players should have more personal instruction, and should be properly guided. It is not enough to have lessons for a few months and then join a band without ever having another private or personal lesson. Good players are not developed in six months or a year—not even in cases where the pupil is possessed of unusual talent. Constant supervision and a systematic course of training will, however, bring about good results.

Most of our youngsters play in bands before they have learned the necessary rudiments of music, or before they have had sufficient instruction. Playing becomes much more simple if it is properly done. The playing of a wind instrument should not be a hardship. It should not require much effort or much exertion, if one has been properly taught. However, the one who has been poorly instructed will never play with ease, nor will he ever acquire a good tone or good intonation.

Music is a moral law. It gives a soul to the universe, wings to the night, flight to the imagination, a charm to sadness, gaiety and life to everything else. It is the essence of order and leads to all that is good, just and beautiful—of which it is the invisible, but nevertheless dazzling, passionate and eternal form.—*Plato*.

Whether one studies singing, violin, or any wind instrument, the most important daily exercise is the practice of long tones. This must be indulged in daily even after one has acquired an embouchure, in order to maintain it. The playing of long tones improves the tonal quality, gives power and endurance, and helps the intonation. The mere fact of having a good ear will not make one play in tune. It is the co-ordination of the ear and the lips that is essential.

Many people have an idea that the person who can play loudest has the best lip control. This is quite erroneous. It is the person who can play softest and who can still control his tones. The person who plays softly and with good tonal quality can also, as a rule, play loudly and make crescendos and decrescendos—and still control his tones. Anyone can play loudly by brute force.

Young bands should be most carefully drilled in slow movements—starting with the simplest kind of hymns and chorals. They should be taught to hold their tones steadily and not get louder or softer unless the music indicates it. Most bands have the very bad fault of chopping off long notes—not giving them their designated value. In a slow movement every note should be given complete value. The tones should be steady. Another important matter is that of breathing. Breath should be taken at the proper places, and not at random. Sometimes there is time for a long deep breath—depending upon the length of phrases that has to be played. At other times, the player must take a short, quick breath. The careful conductor will mark the music, and at rehearsals will explain at what places long or short breaths should be taken. Breath must be taken so as not to take away from the value of the notes or distort the phrasing.

Then careful attention must be paid to the attack. If the entire band sets in on the first beat of the bar, for instance, no tones and no players should be heard individually. The attack should be as clear as though only one person were playing. In order to perfect the attack the conductor should start the band over and over again. Then players themselves must be made to recognize their own faults and shortcomings. If they are not able to do this they will never reach any degree of proficiency. They must also be made to recognize whether or not they are playing out of tune. They must learn to know whether

---

Music is the art directly representative of democracy. If the best music is brought to the people there need be no fear about their ability to appreciate it.
—*Calvin Coolidge.*

they are too sharp or too flat. If they cannot recognize that themselves, they will never play in tune. Slow exercises or pieces will show up all defects very readily.

Phrasing, which for wind instruments consists of slurring or tonguing the proper notes, and taking breath in appropriate places, is another important matter. In the tonguing, one must know whether a sharp tonguing is to be used or a soft, mild one. In a slow movement it should be a soft tonguing. The proper playing of the very simplest hymns and chorals will work wonders with bands. It is through such practice that quality as well as quantity can be achieved. For ear training, for developing a fine style, fine tonal quality, good phrasing, and for giving the players an opportunity to hear and understand their own faults, nothing can be as important or as beneficial. The band that builds on such a foundation is the one that will succeed artistically.

If one wishes to judge the merits of a band, it is only necessary to hear it render a few bars of some slow movement. If it can do that successfully it surely will not have many other faults of great consequence.

Conductors should remember at all times that tone quality should never be sacrificed for volume. A good clear tone carries farther than a loud rough tone. Wind instrument players should not force their tones beyond the power of their control.

Proper playing of slow movements will also teach players what good ensemble playing really means, and that each individual is only a small part of the whole.

Music makes for better citizenship. It will drive out envy and hate, which do so much to poison the well-springs of our life. Whenever our people gather together I would have music, for it brings happiness and contentment.
        —*James J. Davis, Sec'y of Labor in President Harding's Cabinet.*

CHAPTER XIX.

THE PLAYING OF MARCHES

There is nothing quite so inspiring as to hear a spirited march well played by a good band. In fact, it is one of the most thrilling things that can be offered through the medium of music. It is the march that quickens the pulse and makes the blood tingle when a parade passes. It is the march that inspires soldiers to step lightly and with precision. It is the march that makes thousands of soldiers forget fatigue. A march that has a fine rhythmic swing, good melody, snap and pep, will do more for a regiment than all the commands in the world. No orchestra in the world can give to a march the spirit and the thrill that a band can.

It is, of course, much easier to render a march effectively on the platform than on parade, while marching. It is seldom that one ever hears a march well-played for marching purposes. In fact, I confess that I have never heard a really fine marching band. There may be some, but I am free to admit that I never had the good fortune to hear one.

Marching bands have certain very definite hardships to overcome. Playing a wind instrument while marching is in itself a great task. This fact of playing while marching requires considerable practice and experience, and even then it is never quite satisfying. The performer is required to hold his instrument steadily to his lips while playing. This is almost impossible while marching. Then again, the route of march is not generally over the finest concrete roads, such as have been built for automobile traffic. Marching often has to be done over city streets, dirt roads, and on grass, and with the frequent ups and downs, and the bumps, the performer is fortunate if he can keep his mouthpiece to his lips. Successful marching bands have to be schooled and hardened to their work, and must indulge in this type of work frequently in order to do it even passably well.

Music is the servant of everything good, and belongs to the great sisterhood which labors in any and in every form to improve, educate and refine humanity.
—*Andrew Carnegie.*

Our regular Army and Navy Bands naturally have regular daily military duties to discharge, and they, of course, have more marching practice than other types of bands. Unfortunately our Army and Navy Bands are too small for adequate use. During the war these bands were increased to a satisfactory size, but immediately thereafter they were reduced to a size that is not large enough for the finest type of concert music or even for marching purposes. The three service bands in Washington, D. C. (The U. S. Marine Band, U. S. Navy Band. and U. S. Army Band) are probably the only ones that are adequate in size.

As for the National Guard or Militia Bands, there are large and small organizations, but unfortunately they do not have the opportunity of playing together frequently enough. Some of the bands do not rehearse even once a week.

As for the Professional (Civilian) Bands, they can generally be hired to march in parades (with the exception of a few strictly Concert Bands). These Professional Bands, as a rule, do absolutely no military duty. They are not drilled, and as these men have to be paid for rehearsals as well as concerts and other engagements, not much can be expected of such organizations for parade purposes.

I have noticed repeatedly that an Army or Navy band of eighteen or twenty players who are not as efficient as the professionals—will give far better service for parade work than a band of fifty or sixty professionals. In the first place the enlisted men are accustomed to that type of duty and they all work. Most professional bands on parade sound as if only about one-third of the men are actually playing. And this is very frequently the case. The other two-thirds are either resting, or removing the water or saliva which gathers in their instruments. These two excuses are, of course, valid occasionally, but they have been abused to such an extent by players who prefer to loaf than to play, that the band is actually only giving about one-third of what it shculd really be giving. In a long or arduous parade it is necessary in band work for the players to relieve each other occasionally. A cornetist, for instance cannot play a march through twice or even once, without resting. These marches should be rehearsed, and it should be arranged just when and where each player is to be relieved, so that all of a sudden the entire bottom of the band does not drop

---

Rhythm and harmony sink most deeply into the recesses of the soul.—*Plato.*

out. A parade march should be as carefully prepared as a concert march; the marks of precision should be observed and steady rhythm maintained. It is a mistake to play a march as loudly as possible from start to finish. There should be some high spots in parade music too—and in the fortissimo strains everybody should be taking part. The diligent conductor will designate the places in which one player may relieve another so that at no time will his band sound empty.

High School and College Bands frequently have occasion to do parade and marching work, and in fact, marching contests are often held. Some of these bands spend a lot of time rehearsing fancy manoeuvers for special events and do them in a very precise and spectacular manner. Some of these bands are very large, but they seldom sound half their size. The same fault prevails here as with the professional band, although not to such a large degree by any means. The youngsters play for the love of it. When they rest it is because they are fatigued, but this should be taken into account in rehearsal as suggested. Marching bands will improve their performance one hundred percent when the conductor realizes the importance of relieving tired players in a systematic and pre-arranged manner. Good marching bands should be encouraged and far more time should be devoted to this particular phase of band music. The performances of a march for parade should be a work of art.

Until now this chapter has dealt primarily with Marching Bands, but there is much more that can and should be said about the actual playing of the marches themselves. Military Marches are written in ₵ (Alla Breve)—2–4 or 6–8 time, and there is a greater difference between these time designations than most of the players or listeners ever imagine.

In the ₵ (Alla Breve) marches, all quarter notes should be played as though they were eighth notes followed by eighth rests, that is—when they are not slurred. All quarter notes which are not slurred must be played very staccato. Eighth notes are played like sixteenths. Half notes are held for half the bar and the dotted half notes for three-quarters of the bar. Let the long notes be long and the short ones short. It is this contrast that makes for the snappy and spirited effect. Besides giving the notes their proper values, the marks of expression— little accents—pianos—fortes and crescendos should be observed.

Where they sing there let us rest, for wicked people have no songs.—*Luther.*

In the 2-4 March the quarter notes are played in a totally different manner than in the ₵ (Alla Breve) March. In the 2–4 March the quarters are held long (like the halves were held in the Alla Breve March) and the eighths are played staccato when they are not marked with a slur. The dotted eighth in a 2–4 March must be given good value.

The 6–8 March is generally much abused. The quarter notes should *not* be played staccato unless they have a dot over or under them. The dotted quarters (dot following a quarter) should be played long, and, of course, the dotted half note should occupy a full measure. All eighth notes which are not slurred should be played staccato.

In the three types of marches just described, the values of the notes are most essential. The contrast between short and long notes must be marked. It is this contrast which helps make for good rhythm, spirit and dash.

Marches are generally not given enough detailed rehearsal, despite the fact that most bands perform more of them than any other type of music. A Conductor will spend much time on an Overture, an Operatic Fantasie or a Suite at rehearsal, but he will run through a march in the most casual manner, or perhaps even expect the band to read it at sight. This is a grave mistake, and in fact is one of the things that has prejudiced many people against the band. Nothing is too simple or too trivial to be rehearsed carefully. Marches are frequently quite difficult. The band which is carefully rehearsed will always show the results in the performance. A march should be as carefully and thoroughly rehearsed as an Overture.

Rhythm: The first essential in the playing of a March is to be able to maintain a proper and steady rhythm. Naturally this can be achieved through the work of the Conductor—or, on parade, by the Drum Major. If the Conductor does not possess an accurate sense of rhythm (and unfortunately many of them do not) he has no right to lead a band. In most bands it seems as though Bass Drum, Cymbals and Small Drum players take the matter of rhythm into their own hands, and are able to carry all the other players along with them. No conductor of ability or authority will tolerate such a thing. Besides taking the tempo into their own hands, most of the players in the Percussion Section seldom play their parts as they are written, even though their eyes are glued on the music. Drummers can-

I think I should have no other mortal wants if I could always have music.
—*George Eliot.*

not play false notes, for no definite tones can be produced on their instruments, but they can spoil the rhythm or come in on the wrong count. The Percussion Section, more than any other part of the band, must *watch* and *follow* the leader steadily. Good drummers, those capable of playing the music as it is written, and of maintaining a firm rhythm, are very scarce— perhaps more so than players in any other field. I have found this to be true in my own experience. Drummers should be chosen first of all for their sense of rhythm. Every fine drummer should be able to play some other instrument and to read music.

A march without steady and accurate rhythm is like bread without butter. A perfect rhythm must be maintained from start to finish. There should not be the slightest variation in tempo. The use of the metronome at rehearsal is advisable for those conductors who want to be sure that they have the correct rhythm, and maintain it. Rhythm is the first requisite of the conductor.

In Marching Bands, the Drum Major gives the tempo— often very badly. Of course, the Drum Major should be a person of striking physique, but this fine physique should not be the only requisite. He should have a finely developed sense of rhythm, as well as a knowledge of military tactics, and the ability to twirl a baton. It seems as though a satisfactory Drum Major could be selected from among the band players. Many Drum Majors are totally unmusical, and because of their rapid gestures and fast strutting the bands are marched at such a rapid pace that both music and marching are unsatisfactory. Many High School Bands are now headed by girl Drum Majors —some very capable—and others chosen simply for the effective picture they provide.

Tempo: In a March the tempo is a primary requisite. It must be steady and accurate. When played as a concert number, the March is generally played faster than it is for marching purposes, and when played for phonograph records or radio broadcasting these same marches should be played still faster, otherwise they will sound slower when they reach the ears of the listeners. This has been proved by experiment. However, there is a happy medium. It would be a tragedy if some of our bands played their marches as fast as they are frequently heard over the radio. A march is not a galop, and when it is played as such it loses all that it was intended to convey. Many people

---

Music is the highest of all sciences.—*J. S. Bach.*

have an idea that in order to inject spirit and snap into a march it must be played at a galopping pace. This is all wrong and sounds worse than the worst circus or street band.

There are probably more marches than any other type of composition for band and inasmuch as most organizations use marches continually they should assemble the best possible collection of them. As mentioned before, it is the custom of most bands to play a march as an "extra" or encore number after almost every number on its concert program. This is not always a good idea, especially as in most instances the audience is not even given the opportunity of demanding an "encore." Then again, most conductors tire out their players completely before their programs are half over. The lips can only stand so much and no more. In amateur bands, the "embouchure" (lip) of the player is not well enough developed to keep playing steadily. Shorter programs better played, are certainly worth more than long ones poorly played.

Despite the fact that so many fine marches are published, it is strange to see how many conductors still choose ones that are poorly constructed and still more poorly arranged. Every band should have, in its repertoire, a collection of marches that are inspiring, that are well arranged, that are thoroughly rehearsed, and ready for all occasions. Marches should not be too difficult, especially for marching purposes. Conductors should be as careful in the selection of their marches as they are in the selection of the music of the masters. I wish to emphasize, by repeating, the fact that, many of the publications of a decade ago were poorly edited, and were arranged only for very small bands. Sometimes years afterwards, extra parts were added. In many of these older publications the phrasing was wrongly marked, or else not marked at all. We find Cornet and Clarinet parts, which may contain the same notes and the same melodies, not agreeing as to which notes are to be tongued, and which slurred. One may have legato and the other staccato. Even the dynamic markings do not always agree. Under such circumstances, the best band cannot do itself justice. Then again some of the notes are written so small that they are not legible. Very often where two horn parts are printed on one sheet, or two cornet, or two trombone or two clarinet parts, it is quite impossible for the players actually to play what is written. In such instances, the players almost without exception play

Lightlier move the minutes fledged with music.—*Tennyson.*

only the upper notes and as a consequence the full harmony is lacking. This is a very serious matter. Through the influence of the American Bandmasters' Association, the leading publishers have agreed to issue separate and single parts in their band editions, especially the marches that are printed on the small sheets. This has proved a great blessing indeed.

There are many other faults in the playing of band marches. Most marches seem to be all top and bottom, because the middle parts are so badly played, or else not played at all. The first or melody parts are generally more correctly played than the second or third parts. The second and third parts should be as well played as the first in all sections of the band. The leader who thinks that everything is covered up when the melody and bass parts are fairly well played will never have a good band. Second and third Clarinet parts should be carefully studied. The Horn parts and the 2nd and 3rd Cornet parts in Marches are generally the worst played. The Horns are particularly important, since with their "after-beats." they are practically the back-bone of the band. Unfortunately they are seldom even heard. They are too frequently covered up completely by the drums, especially by the "after-beats" of the small Drum. These same drums generally cover up a multitude of badly played and wrong notes in the poorly trained band. It is difficult, even in a first class band, to get good staccato "after-beats" in the horns, which will carry through the band. All the accompaniment and harmony parts of the band should be as carefully and precisely played as the melodic parts. My band uses newly constructed F Alto Horns in the playing of marches so as to get more volume and precision in the after-beats. These are, of course, played by the French Horn players who use the French Horns in all the other music. These new F Altos are played with a French Horn mouthpiece.

Most marches contain what are known as "counter melodies" and these should always be well defined. They most frequently occur in the Trombones and Baritones but occasionally in other instruments as well.

As stated before, detailed attention is seldom paid to the rehearsing of Marches. Much can be done with a March. Attention should be given to tonal balance and tonal quality, just as though it were a work in one of the larger forms. There is a great tendency to overblowing in the playing of Marches.

The power of music all our hearts allow.—*Pope.*

Players exhaust their energy uselessly—for a good clear tone carries much further than a loud rough one. Wind instrument players should never go beyond the limit of a good clear tone at any time. A forced tone never has any value.

Added beauty is given to the March if all the expression marks are carefully observed, and the proper accents accorded the proper notes. Contrast is necessary. There should be soft and loud passages, short and long notes. Many players have a habit of hurrying the music as soon as they see a passage containing a few eighth and sixteenth notes. Such players must be drilled in rhythm. Other players seem to feel that runs or quick passages must be played loudly as well as quickly. Another common fault is the tendency to drag when playing softly. When a phrase or strain is marked "piano" or "forte" the players often perform it in an uneven and jerky manner, giving one note more prominence than another. This serious mistake is very apparent in the playing of marches, and it should be corrected.

Another defect of most bands is that the Clarinet players seldom play forte or fortissimo as the brass instruments increase in volume. The increase in volume is generally from the brasses only. Clarinet players have a tendency to maintain a mezzo-forte quality of tone throughout. They must be urged to participate in the crescendos and loud passages. The desired effects cannot be achieved otherwise.

Saxophones should not "moan" and "weep" in the playing of band music. The Jazz style of "tremolo" is entirely out of place in the Band. Saxophone players seldom play the marches with precision, and especially are they faulty in the playing of staccato notes. The composer does not except the saxophones from the proper playing of their parts, and neither should the conductor. The saxophone, a beautiful instrument, is the most abused of all.

Drummers as a general rule play entirely too loud. Many bands have too many small drums for concert work. Poor drummers can ruin a band, just as good drummers can make a band, to a large degree. A good bass drummer must be quick, alert, responsive to every wish of the conductor. He must know whether to give a long sweeping stroke of the arm or a short stroke of the wrist. He must know whether to hit the drum-head in the center or near the rim; whether a direct stroke or

Everyone should listen to good music several minutes each day.—*John Ruskin.*

just a glancing stroke is needed, and so on. A good drummer will always attract a good deal of attention. Small drummers generally do not play their parts precisely enough. Not many of them are able to play a good "roll." There are many places in Marches where the Cymbals played by hand should be used rather than those attached to the Bass Drum. Most bands have very poor Cymbals. In fact, many of them sound like tin pans. Good Cymbals are rather expensive but they are a fine investment. A ringing Cymbal crash is very effective.

What has been said about Marching Bands applies here too; brass players generally relieve each other in the playing of Marches for concert purposes. But this relieving of one another is seldom done in a systematic way. It seems that each player rests whenever he feels so inclined and frequently two-thirds of the players are resting when the biggest climax occurs. In my own band, I am very strict on this point. I permit one man at each stand in the brass section to rest in the "piano" or "mezzo forte" strains and perhaps occasionally in a "forte" strain, but in most "forte" and in all "double forte" strains every man in the band must play. This gives a proper balance at all times, and when a climax is reached it is a telling one.

Band Contests are held in every state in the Union, and Marches are generally played first as preparatory or "warming-up" pieces. As a rule they are not judged for the contest itself. It is to be hoped that in the near future prizes will be awarded for the best performance of Marches. The proper playing of marches is an art in itself.

A man should hear a little music, read a little poetry, and see a fine picture every day of his life in order that worldly cares may not obliterate the sense of the beautiful which God has implanted in the human soul.—*Goethe*.

A Goldman Band Concert on the Mall in Central Park, New York
(This picture shows only a small part of one of the nightly audiences. It also gives some idea of the beautiful bandstand.)

CHAPTER XX.

OUTDOOR MUSIC

Its Wide Appeal

For open-air performance, there is no contradicting the fact that the band combination of all wind instruments is more easily blended, and the tonal quantity and quality more easily equalized than the orchestral combination of string and wind instruments. Humid or damp weather makes little or no difference in the tone of wind instruments, except perhaps to make them sound more clear, brilliant and easy-blowing—particularly the brasses. Every brass player knows that a new instrument has to be thoroughly moistened inside before it begins to do justice to itself. On the other hand, stringed instruments lose practically all of their resonance in humid or damp weather. And as Berlioz says, even if the number of stringed instruments be doubled, most of their tone is lost in the open. The band, too, can give satisfactory performances indoors, contrary to the belief of many who think that it can only play loudly. The band can render pianissimi almost equal to those of the orchestra, thus enabling it to produce fine dynamic effects. A large number of wood-winds and brasses are a part of every symphony orchestra. These brasses can produce a tumultuous or thundering fortissimo, and who has not heard them produce the most exquisite pianissimo as well? What can be more impressive and grand than the noble brasses in a pianissimo passage? If these effects can be obtained in the orchestra, they can be produced equally well in the band.

Dr. Edward Schaaf, a well-known physician of Newark, N. J., a composer of ability, and a man who has done much to promote open-air music for the people, wrote an article some time ago entitled "The Outdoor Band Concert," from which the following excerpts are quoted:

Wherever there is good music there is harmony. Wherever there is harmony there are good citizens, and therefore we must provide all the good music that is possible.—*J. Hampton Moore* (Mayor of Philadelphia.)

"Of all forms of musical entertainment, none is more popular and none more potent in its cultural effect upon the masses of the people than the open-air band concert.

"Singularly free from the commercial aspect, it is not only altruistic in spirit but thoroughly humanizing in expression and should serve more than it does to arouse and retain the philanthropic interest and support of public-spirited citizens.

"Outdoor concerts by a good band are not only one of the best advertisements a community can have, but also a stimulus to the communal spirit which makes for a better civilization wherever its influence is felt.

"Every city large enough to afford such concerts should make the necessary provisions for supporting them. It is a civic duty, whether it be assumed by individual citizens voluntarily or by the municipality itself. The newspapers reflecting and creating popular sentiment and representing the better element in community thought, should stir up enthusiasm and keep it going until civic spirit is thoroughly awake to the opportunities of pleasure and benefit from free entertainments by high class bands in the beautiful environment of the public parks.

"And what could be nobler, when properly done, than a concert performance of Tschaikowsky's Andante Cantabile (5th Symphony)? What more majestic than such a rendition of the choicest Wagnerian excerpts? What, in the range of solemnity, more inspiring than the Chopin Funeral March played by a high class concert band?

"Band concert music is every bit as noble and inspirational as orchestral music. It can touch the same heights and depths in expressing the lighter or more serious moods of the mind and the eternal longings of heart and soul. Lovers of band music need only consult their own experience to realize the versatility of its appeal, the power it has over the human emotions. In stirring the soul to firm resolve, to high achievement, to courageous action, to supreme devotion, to patriotic sacrifice, it goes beyond any other medium of expression in the whole range of musical art."

It is often wondered why Symphony Orchestras do not reach the masses in the same way that bands reach them. First of all, the orchestras play in halls which cannot hold

---

If we assume that there is in every art a special branch which most adequately represents its character and individuality, it must be admitted that in the art of music that branch is instrumental music.—*Wagner.*

audiences that are large enough to make the concerts pay, unless the price of admission is quite high—too high for the general public. When compared to a band, in the open, the orchestra loses all, or nearly all, of its softer and more delicate passages, and it is almost impossible to maintain a proper tonal balance between the strings and the winds. This makes it possible for ten times, or a hundred times as many people to hear the band to advantage. The fatigued workingman or the tired business man who is shut in all day will be glad to enjoy the fresh air of the park, whereas he would probably rebel against dressing up and sitting in the close atmosphere of the concert hall.

It is not the intention of the author to try to minimize the greatness of the Symphony Orchestra. This cannot be done. The Orchestra has been accepted as an artistic institution for years, whereas the band is not accepted yet in the eyes of many people, for the simple reason that they do not understand the band, and perhaps have never heard a real concert band.

A good band concert does more good for a greater number of people than an orchestra can do. The band has done great missionary work for the orchestra, because most people have heard bands long before they ever attended a symphony concert. Even the smallest city has its "town band." It may not have an orchestra, but the "town band," as poor as it may be, will go out on the village green and make a brave effort to entertain the people. Most of these town bands practice all winter so that they can give a few concerts during the summer. Music with them is a thing of love. The general public prefers a band to an orchestra. It is more thrilling to them. This can be easily proved by the fact that during the past sixty years there has always been one band that has held sway for about thirty years, and was able to tour the United States almost continuously during that period. The first was Patrick Sarsfield Gilmore who toured the United States for many years and made one trip to Europe with his organization. Then came John Philip Sousa, who was an international figure for forty years or more. He not only toured the United States and Canada, year after year, but also made several trips to Europe and one to Cuba, Mexico, Japan, Australia and Africa, all without any financial sponsors. No Symphony Orchestra in the world has ever been able to tour constantly. As a matter of fact, most orchestral tours have been financial failures (even though they generally have

There should be no technic in music which is not music in itself.—*Harold Bauer.*

financial sponsors) while the band tours have been huge successes. I mention these facts simply to show that the band makes a more general and universal appeal, while the orchestra appeals to the few. In his day John Philip Sousa was undoubtedly the best known musician in the world. While every child or grown-up may not have known the name of Beethoven, Wagner or Mozart, with very few exceptions they knew the name of Sousa, in Europe as well as in America. Another bandmaster was destined to succeed Gilmore but after a year or two as Gilmore's successor, he chose to devote his time to composition. This man was Victor Herbert.

There is a mistaken conception among many people that the band is an instrument solely for the open-air. The day will come when our better bands will give seasons of winter concerts just as the orchestras do. It must be admitted that many of the bands of the past had the idea that the one that could be heard at the greatest distance was the best. Only a really fine band can play softly and smoothly. To play softly and sweetly requires more lip control and development than to play loudly. Only a fine player can play with delicacy and control. Some people believed that bands were relegated to out-door performances because they played too loudly to be listened to indoors. Those bands that play too loudly indoors also play too loudly for the open-air.

For out-door performance, the same attention must be given to nuances, phrasing, marks of expression and dynamic markings. It should always be remembered that a soft, clear tone carries further than a loud rough one. Crescendos should be gradual, so that all the strength and power is not spent before the actual climax appears. Crescendos, and descrescendos, are generally too exaggerated as are most accents, ritards and accelerandos. These things are dependent upon the good taste and musicianship of the conductor, and should be carefully worked out at the rehearsals. .

There is no reason in the world why outdoor performances should not be as carefully rendered as those of indoors. Naturally, the question of acoustics enters into the situation, for if there is no suitable stage or bandstand, open-air music is a failure—even with a band. The old style bandstand, open on all sides is quite unsatisfactory. The "Shell" style of band-

Notions may be imported by books from abroad; ideas must be grown at home by thought.—*Hare.*

stand is the proper type. There should be a back sounding-board or shell which extends over the whole band, or at least a large part of it. This will help concentrate the sounds and send them out with a better balance. Much of the success of the acoustics depends upon the position of the bandstand—whether the ground in front slopes or is level, whether there are any buildings nearby, whether there are trees in the close vicinity, and so on. The height of the shell makes a difference too, and whether it is built of wood or stone. It is important that the floor of the stage should not be level. There should be a series of levels or platforms so that each row of musicians is higher that the row in front. This helps the tonal quality, precision, and makes a far better stage picture.

The Goldman Band gives four concerts a week at Central Park in a very beautiful bandstand which is made of limestone. The floor and platform are of wood. The acoustics are excellent, and the large audiences evidently hear the music well, for they sit quietly throughout the concert. No one is permitted to walk in or out of an aisle during the rendition of a number. My band also gives three concerts each week on the Campus at New York University, alongside the Hall of Fame. The bandstand at the University is made of wood. The ground from the band-stand slopes upward, making an almost perfect open-air amphitheatre. The whole effect is beautiful and the acoustics are excellent.

Every city has one or more beautiful parks. Every village has its "green." Every park should have its bandstand, no matter how modest a one it may be, and its band to give concerts. The more music the cities provide, the happier and more contented their people will be. Let music be the means of bringing people together.

To sing seems a deliverance from bondage. Music expresses that which cannot be said, and which cannot be suppressed.—*Victor Hugo.*

CHAPTER XXI.

BAND CONTESTS

The Band Contest idea has spread to every state in the Union, and has become a great factor in the development of bands and band music. It has helped to create an interest in the School Bands, and to create a spirit of rivalry between them. These Contests are very spectacular as well as interesting events.

Each state has its High School Band Contest, and the winner of the state contest is eligible to enter the National High School Band Contest. It has been my privilege to act as Judge, together with John Philip Sousa and other famous bandmasters on many occasions, and I must say that the work which is being accomplished by some of these school bands is simply amazing. There are really fine school bands all over the country, but the largest number of them are to be found in the West and Middle West. They take their bands more seriously than we do in the East, and they give more time and attention to the training of them. The progress which has been made by High School Bands is so remarkable as to seem almost incredible. Within a few years these bands have accomplished so much, that the person who is not familiar with this particular phase of musical activity can scarcely conceive of the advancement that has been made. High School Orchestras, too, have made wonderful strides, but bands have reached greater heights. The band, in many ways, makes a greater appeal to youth. Boys seem to like the flashy wind instruments, the snappy uniforms, the thrill of the parade. The band holds more glamour for the youngsters, and it is, of course, always more spectacular than the orchestra.

The National Band Contests, which are held each year in a different city, are gigantic affairs. They create far more interest than the orchestra contests. Bands are divided into three grades A, B, and C. All bands of Class A are required to

The only reward of virtue is virtue. The only way to have a friend, is to be one. The only people, scientific or other, who never make mistakes are those who do nothing.—*Huxley*.

play what is known as a "warming up" piece—which is not judged. Then they perform the contest piece, which all bands in the same class must play. The third selection is optional. Before each band plays, it is checked up in regard to its instrumentation. The judges then mark the interpretation, tonal quality, intonation, and general effect. The bands then go to another room, or another building and go through a sight reading test. Other judges are assigned for this special purpose. The judges' papers are then turned over to the committee in charge, for final averaging and a report.

Strange things happen at some of these contests, and frequently the bands which the first judges expect to win may be awarded second or third place. They prepared their contest number, and their other program numbers almost faultlessly, but when they went to the judges who marked their sight reading, they lost out. Some bands, of course, work so steadily throughout the year on their contest numbers that they neglect playing enough other music to make them good sight readers. That is most assuredly a mistake. Then again bands that have been carefully trained may lose out because they are lacking in some of the prescribed instruments. Instrumentation counts for a certain number of points. Thus, the band that gives the best performance in regard to interpretation (balance, precision, expression, phrasing, tempo), tonal-quality, intonation, and general effect is not always the one that wins first or second place. Naturally, the spirit of rivalry is very keen, but the fine sportsmanship of the youngsters is generally very apparent. There is as much enthusiasm at one of these contests as there is at a football game, and this speaks well for the cause of music. The day will come when great musical events will be featured on the front pages of our newspapers as prominently as prize fights and other athletic sports

Many bands travel halfway across the country to attend these meets. The money for their transportation and other expenses is generally raised by the proud citizens of their town, or by the leading civic organizations. Naturally, they expect their band to come back with the laurels. The losing bands frequently do feel discouraged. It is for this reason that many cities and states are now organizing huge Music Festivals rather than Contests. In the festivals the spirit of rivalry is lacking,

Never put off until tomorrow what you can do today. Never spend your money before you have earned it. Never buy what you don't need because it is cheap.
—*Thomas Jefferson.*

so that there cannot be any bitter feeling afterwards. My personal belief is that both the Contest and the Festival ideas have advantages to offer. They are both to be encouraged. The contests have certainly promoted the cause of bands and have inaugurated a spirit of rivalry which must exist if advancement is to be made. The festivals, too, have brought together large numbers of bands, for the sheer joy of playing, and for the good of the art.

At the contests the bands generally parade through the streets, where marching is judged. Military officers generally are selected for this work, but this contest is separate from the purely musical one. The idea of the marching band contest is a very worthy one, for good marching and playing bands are so very rare. One bad feature of these contests in the past, however, has been that the bands have on several occasions had to do their marching shortly before playing off their "finals" for concert honors. Playing while marching is very difficult at best, and also tiring. The marching should not be done too near the concert contest time, as it is too tiring for the youngsters and places too much strain on their lips.

As has already been stated, each band at the contests is permitted to play a short "warming up" piece of its own selection. This is generally a march. My observation has been that the march is seldom played with as much precision or effect as the required contest piece. This is probably due to the fact that the leader realizes that the playing of the march is not judged. It is a serious mistake, however, not to take pains in the rehearsing of all numbers that are publicly performed. Some leaders select marches of poor quality that are not well arranged. Others select difficult ones that are not really effective. The second number is the prescribed contest piece which every band must play. This composition is chosen by the Music Committee in charge of the contest. The contesting bands generally prepare this piece with great care, although it is surprising to see how varied are the interpretations of the conductors. There is no excuse for any conductor of ability not knowing the tempo of the music he is conducting, especially as the test piece is usually some standard or classical composition, and there is also no reasonable excuse for the conductor not knowing the traditional interpretation of the music. If he is a

---

None but the well-bred man knows how to confess a fault, or acknowledge himself in an error.—*Benjamin Franklin.*

student, he will find a way of getting all the information he requires, from a good recording, the radio, or a competent symphony orchestra. And if all of these methods are impossible for one reason or another, bandmasters can seek information from those who know. No bandmaster should be too proud to seek information regarding compositions with which he is not familiar. In fact, no bandmaster should attempt to conduct a composition unless he feels thoroughly convinced that his understanding of it is correct. It has always been my opinion that at these contests the bandmasters were being judged, and not the bands, and in the final analysis that is the case. When judging interpretation, balance, precision, expression, phrasing and tempo, who is being judged? The conductor—by all means—for he is solely responsible for all of these items. The conductor is also responsible to a great degree for the tonal effect, and as for the general effect, that too is solely up to him.

The third and last piece on the contest program is generally an optional piece, and each band prepares what its leader selects. This closing piece has to be judged. Too frequently works are selected which are beyond the capabilities of the players. This again is the fault of the leader. In most instances the closing number is too long, especially when it is considered that each band has to play three pieces. It takes two or three days to hear all the bands. The Committee in charge should regulate the time allotment for each piece.

Band Contests and Band Festivals have become an institution in this country and they have already made their importance and their benefit felt.

Wink at small faults; remember thou hast great ones.—*Benjamin Franklin.*

CHAPTER XXII.

MASSED BANDS

Performances by Massed Bands have become quite frequent of late, but unfortunately are rarely successful. Quantity does not insure quality, and as a rule, these large massed bands are so enormous that they become very unwieldy.

Massed Band performances can be made very stirring—very thrilling, if they are prepared with care and thought. It is not satisfactory to bring together from two to fifty bands for a performance without a rehearsal, without the proper placing of the various choirs of instruments, and without regard for tonal balance.

Several times during the past few years I have conducted massed bands ranging in size from one hundred and fifty to twenty-five hundred or more players, and I must confess that the performances have generally been very unsatisfactory. The massed band performance is usually staged as the spectacular climax of a Band Contest or Music Festival. The prevailing custom has been to throw a huge mass of players together and create a picture that is pleasing to the eye but not so pleasant to the ear. In most of these performances, each band goes in as a unit, one band being placed next to the other. Good results cannot possibly be achieved in such a manner. This would mean that the bass drummer of one band would be near the conductor, while another bass drummer would be a block away to the right and a third one almost a quarter of a mile away to the left, and others still further away to the center and rear. By no stretch of the imagination would these performers be able to beat their drums in unison; so from the very outset, no rhythm could be maintained. The various distances at which the players are placed plays havoc with a performance. The eye is quicker than the ear—and in performances where large numbers of players are involved, this is an important factor.

A man has no claim upon his fellow creatures beyond bread and water and a grave, unless he can win it by his strength or skill—*Nathaniel Hawthorne.*

To achieve satisfactory results, bands should lose their identity for massed performances, that is to say, the massed bands should be seated as any individual band would be, with all the Flutes together, Clarinets together, Cornets together, and so on. Imagine the basses being scattered to the North, East, South and West, and frequently several hundred feet apart. Or think of an important trombone passage being played by performers in as many different directions and just as widely separated. Good renditions under such circumstances are impossible.

In advance of each Massed Band performance, a chart of the seating arrangement should be drawn. If the various instruments are properly grouped, they should also be properly balanced, if artistic results are desired. If the massed band embodies a hundred saxophones and only fifty clarinets it will readily be seen that tonal balance will be uneven as well as unsatisfactory. If there are one hundred and fifty trombones and only seventy-five cornets and trumpets, the effect will also be anything but satisfying. Massed bands should be composite in their makeup—and properly balanced in regard to the number of instruments of each type. This is the first requisite for success. The second essential is the proper placing of the various sections of players.

Where such large groups of players are concerned, they must be brought as near to the conductor as possible, and placed so that they can see his baton clearly. If the group is in excess of seven hundred or a thousand it is often advisable to group the players in a circle with the conductor in the center. This brings the players closer, even though some of them see only his back most of the time. Naturally, much depends upon the place of performance—whether indoors or in the open—and also upon the acoustical qualities of the place. Much of the sound is lost in the open, especially where there is no proper background, or when there is no wooden floor. Where the players are all on an even level, it is more difficult to achieve good results. When the playing takes place on open fields—on the grass—much of the fine tonal quality and brilliancy of the band is lost. Where the massed bands are unusually large, it is a good idea to have the various bandmasters stationed about fifty or sixty feet apart, facing the conductor, and ready for any emergency; although if these bandmasters are not very ac-

---

To follow foolish precedent, and wink with both our eyes, is easier than to think.
—*Cowper.*

curate and alert, such a procedure could also work to great disadvantage. The bandmasters should be placed at various positions, however, to help enforce proper discipline and to carry out the plans that have been prepared. There should be a chief whose duties would be to prepare and arrange the purely physical side of the undertaking so that everything would be in complete readiness when the conductor takes up his baton. The handling of these bands and the placing of the players, and the discharging of them after the concert should be accomplished with military precision.

In the placing of the players, the drums should be placed in the center, not too far away from the conductor. The basses should be placed likewise. Unless these two fundamental sections are properly placed the performance will be a shabby one. For the playing in general, only one or two drums should be used, but for special solo effects or climaxes, the entire percussion section can be used to good advantage. These details should be prepared or rehearsed in advance. With all the drums pounding away steadily, the rhythm is apt to be uneven, and all stirring effects and climaxes lost.

And now the question arises, "Which music is most suitable for massed band performance?" This depends largely upon the number of players, the place of the performance—and the opportunity for rehearsing.

It is a proved fact that the playing of marches does not always give the best results in massed band playing, when the band is extremely large. It is much more difficult to maintain a steady rhythm, and keep things properly together in a march (or other fast movement) than it is in a slow movement. Some marches are particularly good for massed band performances, while others, which may be excellent marches, are for one reason or another not at all appropriate for these large combinations of instruments. Music chosen for such performances must be carefully and wisely chosen. Slow movements, in a "Moderato" or "Andante" tempo can usually be rendered with much finer effect than can faster music. The eye and the ear have a better opportunity to synchronize properly.

To my mind there should be some specially written compositions for massed bands, and I have already asked some composers to undertake the writing of such works. Most of the massed band playing I have heard in the past, has consisted

---

Speaking generally, no man appears great to his contemporaries, for the same reason that no man is great to his servants—both know too much of him.—*Colton.*

mainly of a huge volume of sound, mostly noise. Many compositions which were used were totally unsuited to such a purpose,
and seemed to be chosen without any rhyme or reason. Some
very wonderful and thrilling effects can be achieved with massed
bands, but *not* by having the entire ensemble play steadily.
Why not show what can be done effectively? Why not have a
composition which starts with the low reeds, then gradually
adds the clarinets, the flutes, piccolos, oboes, etc., then the
horns, cornets, trumpets, each section, one after the other until
a huge climax is reached, in which the entire percussion section
can join to advantage. This would give an idea of the tonal
qualities of the various sections and the tonal balance and blending. Starting with only a few instruments and building up
section by section until the entire band is in action would
create a climax to thrill any audience. Massed band playing
can be raised to a higher and more artistic level. Many wonderful effects can be achieved, effects which no orchestra can possibly accomplish. The past has given us quantity of tone, rather
than quality. Too little detailed attention has been given to
the subject of Massed Bands and to the music which they perform.

Conceit in weakest bodies strongest works.—*Shakespeare.*

CHAPTER XXIII.

BAND CAMPS

One of the latest developments along the line of musical activity is the Band and Orchestra Camp—or in some instances the strictly Band Camp. When the first camp of this kind was organized a few years ago, musicians were doubtful of its success and frowned upon the idea. These camps, however, have demonstrated their right to exist, and, as a matter of fact, they are now a great factor in the musical uplift of the youngsters of the country. It was my great pleasure and privilege to visit two of these camps in the summer of 1932, one at Interlochen, Michigan (The National Music Camp), where I conducted the closing band concert of the season, and one at Oakland, Maine (Eastern Music Camp), where I performed a similar service. Last summer, 1933, I visited the Ernest Williams Band Camp at Saugerties, New York. I also visited Camp Wainwright at La Grange, Ind. What I heard, and what I saw at these Camps convinced me that they were very worthwhile institutions. They afford opportunity for boys and girls to get the benefit of private instruction on all instruments during a period of eight weeks, under teachers of authority and renown. They also get the benefit of band, orchestra and choral practice. They take lessons in musical theory, harmony, and counterpoint. Several series of concerts are given. Besides the musical benefits there are the usual athletic and out-door activities which are always identified with camp life.

These camps offer the finest cultural advantages, and their supervision is all that can be desired. The youngster is fortunate indeed who is privileged to spend a summer in such environment, for besides securing fine personal instruction, he has the opportunity of gaining excellent musical routine and experience plus health-building athletic activities. The Camp fees seemed to me very moderate, and among the very fine features of the

---

We all like the man who "sticks through thick and thin."—*Abraham Lincoln.*

enterprise are the full and part scholarships which are awarded to worthy students who cannot afford full fees.

Such men as Dr. Walter Damrosch, John Philip Sousa, Ossip Gabrilowitch, Frederick Stock, Dr. Howard Hanson, Percy Grainger, Dr. Carl Busch, Henry Verbrugghen, and other famous musicians have visited one or more of these camps and have acted as guests conductors; all were greatly impressed with what they saw and heard.

There are also other very worthwhile Music Camps throughout the country which are doing the very highest type of work. These camps should be encouraged in every possible way, for they have opened up a new system of summer musical instruction, and have created an additional source of income to teachers.

The equipment at the camps I have visited has been without exception remarkable. There were concert stages for outdoor performances which would do credit to any large city, and the acoustics were all that could be desired.

Your friend is the man who knows all about you and still likes you.—*Anon.*

PART III.

CHAPTER XXIV.

SAXOPHONES

The Saxophone is or can be a very beautiful-toned instrument, but it is the most abused instrument the world has ever known. The inventor (Sax) never dreamed that his invention would be as popular as it is today, nor did he believe it would be so maligned.

The Saxophone is made of brass and is conical in its tubing. It is played with a single reed like a clarinet, therefore the tonal quality is really more influenced by the reed; in comparison with the clarinet, it is somewhat nasal. It belongs to the reed family. It is a beautiful and useful instrument even though its compass is somewhat limited. The tone blends well with the reeds or the brasses, since it partakes of the nature of both. Saxophones may be used to advantage for solo, melodic, or accompanying purposes.

The Saxophone is one of the easiest (perhaps the easiest) of all wind instruments to play, and that, perhaps, is the cause of the great abuse of it. Gilmore used Saxophones in his band, but nowhere else were they used in our country, to any noticeable extent, until the advent of the Jazz Band. Then the Saxophone became a craze in America, and almost all over the world. The craze continued to such an extent that some factories devoted their efforts almost exclusively to the manufacture of these instruments. Many musicians referred to them as instruments of torture, and they were that in the hands of some players. But I say again, the Saxophone can be a beautiful and worthwhile instrument.

When the Jazz craze started, almost everyone wanted this sort of novelty, and when it was learned that the fingering was not very complicated and that a fair embouchure or lip development could be secured more quickly on this than on any other

---

Be what nature intended you for, and you will succeed. Be anything else and you will be ten thousand times worse than nothing.—*Sydney Smith.*

reed instrument, the Saxophone became even more popular. Jazz Bands sprang up by the hundreds. The whole country seemed Jazz mad. Jazz Bands became busier than any other type of organization. It was a simple matter for any clarinet player to learn the Saxophone. Almost every bad clarinet player, who could not make a living with the clarinet, became a Saxophone player. These bad clarinet players made bad saxophone players too, but at least most of them were able to earn a livelihood, during the years of plenty. The craze has died out as it was bound to do.

A quartet of Saxophones is an asset to any band. A quintet is better still. The Saxophone family consists of the following instruments: Soprano, Alto, Tenor, Baritone and Bass. The Soprano is seldom used since it seems to be the most difficult to play in tune. Few players have mastered it, but then few players seem to have mastered any of the others either. The greatest fault is that these instruments are seldom played in tune, because most of the players have never studied or practiced enough to have an embouchure or lip control, and because their ears are not well enough trained. Their tonal quality suffers for the same reason. As a consequence, the Saxophone has not merited the serious consideration which it deserves. There is no earthly reason why this instrument should be played so much more out of tune than any other.

Most players acquire a tremolo tone which cannot be tolerated in a fine band. This comes from trying to "weep" and "moan" in the playing of Jazz music, and trying to "croon" and imitate "laughing Jackasses," "crying hyenas," "neighing horses," and "mooing cows," not to mention "buzzing mosquitoes," "bumble bees," and hundreds of other animals and sounds. When the saxophone is used more as a musical instrument, and studied and practiced properly, it will be respected as it deserves to be. More legitimate Saxophone players will receive a warm welcome in the near future.

Saxophone players have been taboo in many fine organizations of the legitimate type, because they are not accustomed to playing accurately. Moaning and weeping, laughing and shaking are not required in the music of the masters, or in lighter music of a standard type.

The world generally gives its admiration, not to the man who does what nobody else ever attempts to do, but to the man who does best what the multitude does well.—*Macaulay.*

We want and need the Saxophone by all means, but we also want many more players to study it seriously, and not to treat it merely as a trick instrument.

Another drawback of the Saxophone is the fact that some of the players play on three or four different instruments of the Saxophone family, then also dabble on the Clarinet, Alto Clarinet, Bass Clarinet, Oboe, Bassoon, and others. Most of our good wind instrument players have all they can do to maintain their artistry and control of any one instrument. It is quite impossible to acquire an embouchure or lip control so that one can play three, four, five or six different wind instruments with good tonal quality or accurate intonation.

The works of those who have stood the test of ages have a claim to that respect and veneration to which no modern can pretend.—*Sir Joshua Reynolds*.

THE CELEBRATED ITALIAN COMPOSER,
OTTORINO RESPIGHI AND EDWIN FRANKO GOLDMAN

CHAPTER XXV.

THE CORNET AND TRUMPET

DIFFERENCES BETWEEN THE TWO INSTRUMENTS
USES AND ABUSES OF EACH

My reason for writing this chapter is that these instruments—the Cornet and the Trumpet—suffer great abuse in many ways. Many performers are doing themselves a great injustice through not understanding the differences between the two instruments, and in many instances are neglecting the one that would be more serviceable to them and on which they might be able to achieve better results and greater success.

The Cornet and the Trumpet, while they are similar in many respects, are instruments vastly different in tonal quality. Both are important factors in the music of today, and neither could possibly be dispensed with. There seems, however, to be a great difference of opinion regarding the relative merits of each. Unfortunately, many performers do not know the difference between the two instruments, and as a consequence they frequently labor under serious disadvantage. It would be to the advantage of all players and all prospective performers to study the merits of each and to learn which would best serve their purpose. Each instrument is important in its own sphere and the player should know the benefits and effects to be obtained through each.

The Trumpet is, of course, the older instrument, and was used in various forms for centuries before it assumed its present shape and quality. The Cornet, which came into use only in the nineteenth century, when valves were first applied to wind instruments, is a modification of the Trumpet. After the Cornet was somewhat perfected it became a very popular instrument, particularly in England and America. In America it was used for many years to the entire exclusion of the Trumpet. Every soloist of renown, including Jules Levy, M. Arbuckle, A. Liberati,

---

A man never sees all that his mother had been to him till it's too late to let her know that he sees it.—*W. D. Howells.*

Walter Emerson, Theodore Hoch, Herbert L. Clarke, Ernest Williams, Del Staigers, Walter Smith, Frank Simon, and others, rendered his solos on the Cornet. Up to thirty-five years ago, the Trumpet was practically unknown here, and the Cornet was used in all the symphony orchestras of the country and even at the Metropolitan Opera House in New York. In those days the country was very young musically, and we did not boast as many symphony orchestras as we do today. It was about 1897 that the larger orchestras began to adopt Trumpets instead of Cornets. One or two orchestras used Trumpets previous to this. I recollect this very well because I joined the Metropolitan Opera House Orchestra about that time and was told that I would have to provide myself with a Trumpet—an instrument which I had never used before. Our American factories made few or no trumpets in those days. The Symphony and Grand Opera Orchestras made a step in the right direction when they adopted the Trumpet, because it is the proper instrument for that particular type of music, and because the composers' scores call for Trumpets.

With the advent of the Trumpet in our large orchestras, a demand was created for this instrument, and within a few years practically every Cornet player was casting aside his instrument in favor of the Trumpet—in most instances for no valid reason.

The Bb Trumpet and the Bb Cornet contain precisely the same amount of tubing, although the Trumpet is longer than the Cornet in appearance. The tubing of the Trumpet is differently distributed, and the bore is somewhat different; this results in a different quality of tone. The compass and register of both instruments are identical, and they differ principally in tonal quality, due to the difference in bore and tubing and to the different style of mouthpiece, which is an important item. The Cornet is conical in about two-thirds of its tubing length, and cylindrical in one-third. Its tubing is also somewhat wider. The Cornet mouthpiece is not as long as that of the Trumpet and its cup is considerably deeper. The Trumpet has long narrow tubing, cylindrical in about two-thirds of its length, and conical in the other third. (Conical means having the form of a cone, round and tapering—cylindrical means that the tubing has the same diameter throughout and does not taper.) The

It is often better to have a great deal of harm happen to one than a little; a great deal may rouse you to remove what a little will only accustom you to endure.
—*Greville.*

Trumpet mouthpiece is longer than that of the Cornet and its cup is shallower.

Few people realize that though the Bb Trumpet is a longer instrument than the Bb Cornet, they both contain the same amount of tubing. If the main tubing of either instruments (exclusive of the three valve slides) were straightened out it would be found to be about fifty-three and one-quarter inches long. This applies to low pitch instruments. The spread of the bell might make a slight difference, but this wouldn't be very noticeable. In order to attain the proper pitch the above-mentioned length of tubing is imperative. Trumpet tubing is, as a rule, about an inch shorter, but this is made up in the trumpet mouthpiece, which is longer. The Cornet is shorter because it contains more bends in the tubing.

The Trumpet is the instrument that is used in the Symphony and Grand Opera Orchestra because the composer's score generally calls definitely for the Trumpet. There are, of course, many instances where the composer writes a work which is scored for Trumpets and Cornets. For instance, many of the French Operas of Massenet and Meyerbeer call for two Trumpet parts as well as two Cornet parts. The Trumpet is better adapted to the needs of the Symphony Orchestra than the Cornet. Its tone is thinner, more piercing and perhaps more brilliant than that of the cornet. Berlioz has said that "The quality of tone of the Trumpet is noble and brilliant; it suits with warlike ideas, with cries of fury and vengeance, and with songs of triumph; it lends itself to the expression of all energetic, lofty and grand sentiments and to the majority of tragic accents. It may even figure in a jocund piece, provided the joy assumes a character of impulse or of pomp and grandeur." The trumpet is also effective where the music assumes a militant character or where a fanfare effect is to be obtained. Trumpet parts are not given as much melody nor as many florid passages as are given to the Cornet. As mentioned before, the Trumpet is used to a greater extent today than the Cornet. It would be wise indeed if many of the players who now play Trumpet would take up the Cornet instead, because in many of the smaller combinations, that is, in the smaller orchestras which devote their energies to popular and jazz music, the Cornet would be a more satisfactory instrument than the Trumpet. The Cornet is more ideally suited for home or parlor use. It is,

Take away from our hearts the love of the beautiful, and you take away the charm of life.—*Rousseau.*

of course, possible for all Trumpet players to play the Cornet and for all Cornet players to play the Trumpet. In dance and jazz orchestras where many players perform on two, three or more instruments, it might be a good idea for Trumpet players occasionally to change to the Cornet because in much of the music they render the Cornet would give better results. It is most important, however, that the proper mouthpiece be used for each instrument. When the cornet is used, a cornet mouthpiece should be used, and vice versa. It is possible to get a combination cornet and trumpet mouthpiece with a removable rim. In this case the embouchure of the player will not be affected. Many Trumpet players who find they cannot obtain the desired smoothness and lightness in their playing will find that they will have more success on the cornet.

The Trumpet mouthpiece is a most important item. Many players are in the habit of using a Cornet mouthpiece on a Trumpet. This is a very serious mistake indeed as the instrument under these conditions has neither the proper Trumpet tone nor the proper Cornet tone.

My contention is that the Trumpet should be used for music that has a Trumpet nature and that is written specially for it, and that the Cornet should be used for all other purposes. This does not mean that the Trumpet cannot be used satisfactorily in smaller combinations. It simply means that the Cornet would be more satisfying. Conductors should give more time and thought to this subject.

Trumpets should be used in every large orchestra and in every band, but in bands there should be Cornets as well as Trumpets, and the Cornets should play at least the first two parts. Many of our bands are now using Trumpets exclusively. This is a serious mistake.

The Cornet itself is a cross between the Trumpet and the Fluegelhorn. Its tone is less piercing and bright than that of the Trumpet and less mellow and veiled than that of the Fluegelhorn. The Cornet is tremendously popular as a solo instrument and as such is far more satisfactory than the Trumpet. As mentioned above, all of the great soloists achieved their fame and success on the Cornet. The Cornet is in some ways easier to manipulate than the Trumpet, particularly in legato and technical passages. It has far more flexibility and is more adapted to facile passages. The Cornet has a great re-

---

Do good to thy friend to keep him, to thy enemy to gain him.—*Benjamin Franklin.*

semblance to the human voice and it is for that reason that it makes such a universal appeal. In band transcriptions it will be found that vocal (soprano) parts are generally assigned to the Cornet.

The Cornet mouthpiece is deep. This, together with the larger bore of the instrument, helps to produce a broader and thicker tone. It is a great mistake to use a Trumpet mouthpiece on a Cornet, as many players are in the habit of doing. In the band the Cornet always takes the solo part and in all good arrangements there should be special parts for the Trumpet.

Unfortunately, many people purchase the Trumpet because they believe it looks better than the Cornet. It is my honest opinion that beginners would do better to take up the Cornet first, and later the Trumpet if desired. In conclusion, I wish to state again that both instruments have their individual uses and advantages and that both instruments have been greatly abused. At the present time, the Trumpet is abused by being substituted in places where a Cornet would be more satisfactory. The Cornet is abused through neglect. The Cornet must and will come back.

Good Trumpet players are plentiful today, but fine Cornet players are scarce, particularly Cornet soloists. Fame and fortune await the capable Cornet soloist of the future.

No great genius is without an admixture of madness.—*Aristotle.*

CHAPTER XXVI.

THE CORNET SOLOIST

The cornet soloist has greater opportunities than most other wind players. The instrument is one that can be used for almost all purposes and under all conditions, and that is wherein its popularity lies. In band music it takes the principal part; in orchestra music it is very essential. For open-air work no other instrument is its equal. When played with the organ in church, its effect is truly inspiring. For use as a parlor instrument, it is highly effective for interpreting songs, and rendering almost any vocal music. To stir a vast crowd to enthusiasm, the cornet can always be counted upon. For material purposes, or to attract the attention of the multitude, the bright clear tones of the cornet will create the desired effect. These are some of the reasons that have helped to make the cornet such a favorite. With these things in his favor from the outset, the cornetist really has an advantage over the players of other wind instruments, and if he makes use of his numerous opportunities, an interesting and successful career awaits him.

Fifty or sixty years ago, when the cornet began to receive its first recognition as a solo instrument, performers were in such demand that there was not a sufficient supply. This was at the time when Levy, Arbuckle, Liberati and Emerson were in their prime. Every prominent band in those days made an effort to feature some great soloist, and even the orchestras entered into this unusual rivalry. For a time it looked as though the cornet would crowd many of the other solo instruments out. These artists achieved international fame and were rivals for honors. Their rivalry was a great stimulus for better and finer work on the part of each. Levy probably achieved more fame than the others and was a "star" in every sense of the word. His name was advertised as prominently as that of Adelina Patti and Jenny Lind, the world-renowned singers, and in his day he was as popular an idol as Caruso was later on.

Trouble springs from idleness, toil from ease.—*Benjamin Franklin.*

This may seem strange to many of the present generation, but it is true nevertheless. The announcement that one of the prominent cornet soloists was to appear was ample guarantee that the concert would be a financial success. While Arbuckle and Liberati never quite achieved such tremendous popularity, they were also wonderful performers and became world-famous.

I have often been asked whether we have as many fine artists today, and whether the opportunity is as great. In answer to the first question I will say that we have many extraordinary players today, some few who are world-famous, others who are nationally famous, and still more who have achieved only local fame. The one who is known only locally may be a fine artist, and that he is not better known may be due either to the fact that he has never had an opportunity or that he did not grasp the opportunity when it was presented. The opportunity is as great today as ever before, and to my mind even greater. In the first place there are more concerts, more capable teachers and last, but not least, more people who like music. This last is an all-important item because the soloist must have an audience. It is perhaps true that our audiences expect more now than they did years ago, because people are becoming more and more accustomed to hearing good music well rendered. They are now able to discriminate between an artist and an inferior player. The demands upon the soloist are therefore much greater. To begin with, the performer who wants to achieve success must choose a number that has merit, and then render it artistically.

It is sad to relate that one of the most serious drawbacks the soloist has to contend with is the lack of good compositions for the instrument. There was a time when the public would listen to almost anything, but nowadays they generally demand the best. Formerly any kind of "clap-trap" triple-tongue Polka was applauded, and some of these so-called compositions were positively offensive to anyone possessing any musical feeling. I believe the time will come when our great composers will find it worth their while to write cornet solos, just as they write music for the violin, piano and voice today. The more artistic cornet players we develop and the sooner we can prove to the world at large that cornetists are as serious in their aims and ambitions as other musical students, the sooner will the

---

The art of being able to make a good use of moderate abilities wins esteem and often confers more reputation than real merit.—*La Rochefoucauld.*

composers be assured that writing for the cornet would prove a success for the performer and writer alike. If our composers realized, for instance how many cornetists there are in the United States alone, they would probably soon be convinced that it might be to their advantage to give this instrument some attention. Of course, we have better cornet literature now than ever before, much of which consists of original compositions, transcriptions and arrangements of one kind or another, but actual cornet solos from the pens of masters are a rarity.

The soloist who is desirous of building up a repertoire has a large assortment from which to choose despite the fact that the masters have not written much for the instrument. If performers will be careful to choose solos that vary in style they will be able to move any audience to enthusiasm. A few good Fantasies with variations, some high-class songs (religious and secular) and a few well-known ones to be used as encores, are all that are necessary. The Fantasies will serve to display one's technic, while the songs and arias will show the tonal quality, style, and phrasing to good advantage. The successful soloist is entitled to whatever honor and reward he achieves, as the money he receives can never repay him in full for his years of conscientious study and many sacrifices. The real artist gives the best years of his life to his work. When rendering a solo he gives free rein to his emotions, and infuses as much of his personality into the performance as is consistent with good taste. He takes no undue liberties with the music but tries his utmost to render it as the composer intended it, realizing that he is only the means through which the composer expresses his idea. He studies each work thoroughly in order to ascertain its true worth and meaning, and to get whatever good effects are possible. The marks of expression are carefully adhered to and he endeavors to get into the spirit of the piece. When a solo has been prepared in this manner it will be rendered musically and in a refined and elegant style.

Besides having the ability to perform his solos properly the soloist must, of course, possess other essential personal qualities. If he wishes to surge forward he must have some business ability, too, and not rely solely upon his playing. He must be prompt, and reliable at all times in his business dealings. In appearance he should be a model of neatness, for looks count for much with an audience. His standing position should be

One of the winning forces in life consists in being handicapped.—*Madison C. Peters.*

graceful, and he must hold the cornet in a pleasing manner. Applause should be acknowledged with dignity, modesty and appreciation. On the stage, the soloist should be free from any uncalled for mannerisms. Encores should be graciously rendered, if there is a generous and sufficient demand. The cultivation of grace in stage deportment in all particulars should be carefully developed. Last, but not least, the performer who desires to become popular and wishes to maintain his popularity must possess an interesting personality. He should have some magnetism and be able to make and keep friends. He cannot afford to be haughty or to belittle the efforts of others.

It has always appeared to me that our American students are particularly well adapted to the cornet, and since we have had so many remarkable players in the past there is no reason why we should not have many more and perhaps greater ones in the future. We must look to the students of today for the artists that are to be.

It never rains roses; when we want more roses, we must plant more bushes.
—*George Eliot.*

CHAPTER XXVII.

OTHER SOLO INSTRUMENTS

There is no reason why the cornet should have a monopoly of the solos played with the band. Other instruments are also capable of giving good results when properly played. Of course, the main difficulty lies in the fact that most band concerts are given in the open air, and this eliminates some of the woodwind instruments from consideration. However, if the band is playing in a shell or other device which intensifies the carrying power of the instruments, even these are feasible.

The woodwind instruments have a much larger body of good music to choose from than have the brasses. The great masters frequently wrote sonatas, concertos and other solos for flute, clarinet and oboe. Some of these do not, for many reasons, lend themselves to use as solos with band. In some instances, they are too long, and the accompaniments do not lend themselves to band transcription. But there are hundreds of shorter pieces which make admirable solos for such a purpose. These show off the beauties of the instruments and give opportunity for technical display while retaining at the same time, the dignity of good music. For indoor concerts, what could be more agreeable than a solo rendered on the flute, oboe, clarinet or horn?

Brass instruments in general suffer from the scarcity of good music written for them. This is unfortunately true of the cornet as it is of the others. Yet cornet solos are popular, and there is little reason therefore why solos by trombone or baritone players should not be well received. Even the tuba has on occasion been used as a solo instrument. All of the brasses carry well in the open. There are several good numbers written for a trio of cornets, or for a quartet or quintet made up of

The man who cannot stand to have his plans and ideas criticized is a fool. The wise men welcome criticism, so long as it is honest and intelligent. I know, and you do, men who want no one about that does not agree with them, men who are afraid of being told unpleasant truths. Such men are fools. In a long journey, as Emerson says, "The truth, however unpleasant, is the safest traveling companion."
—*Theodore Roosevelt.*

various brass instruments, and various combinations of reed and mixed ensembles. These can be very effective when well performed, and they should provide a welcome note of variety.

With the development in this country of so many excellent players of wind instruments, it is to be hoped that composers of note will turn their attention to the composition of some new and worthwhile solos for all the different wind instruments. This would give great impetus not only to solo playing, but to the entire band movement as well.

He who sets limits to himself will always be expected to remain within them.
—*Schumann.*

CHAPTER XXVIII.

SUITABLE SOLOS AND HOW TO PLAY THEM

BUILDING A REPERTOIRE

Solos for nearly all wind instruments are published in vast quantities as well as in large varieties, but in most instances players do not choose solos that are suited to their capabilities or their own individual style of playing. In fact, it seems to be the ambition of most performers to gather the most difficult music that is procurable, whether they are able to play it or not. It is, of course, a laudable desire to want to be able to play music that requires technical skill and mastery, but too many waste valuable time trying to perform solos that are far beyond their reach. The result is that they not only fail to accomplish their aim, but also retard their progress to a great extent. The beginner who takes a few lessons and then goes ahead without the aid of a teacher, invariably thinks he is ready for any kind of a solo after a short while. It does not matter much to him whether his embouchure is steady and reliable, or whether he has the necessary command of execution. As long as he is able to blurt out the notes in some manner or other, even though they are devoid of all surety and rhythm, he seems to be satisfied that he has accomplished something. Whether the high notes respond freely, or whether they have to be blasted out by sheer brute force seems to make no difference.

Too many players try to perform solos that are beyond their capabilities, and the result is always miserable. They do not play these solos, but in truth "play at them."

If each player would be willing and satisfied to adhere to music that is within his reach and grasp, what different results would be obtained! In this manner he could render whatever is attempted in a worthy and satisfactory manner, and derive some benefit from his efforts. Such music could be studied thoroughly, and the details mastered. It surely is torture to try to accomplish something that is impossible, and the player who tries to render a solo that is beyond him, not alone tor-

---

It is not doing the thing we like to do, but liking the thing we have to do, that makes life blessed.—*Goethe*.

tures himself, but everyone who is compelled to hear him as well. Is it a pleasant sight to see a person play as if he were performing the most awful form of physical labor? Or is it nice to have the feeling that everytime a high note is to be played, a blood vessel may burst? The player who is wise and prudent will include in his repertoire only such solos as he is able to master and render with a degree of surety. The very difficult solos are meant to display the performer's technic, and it takes years of careful and patient study to master the technic of any instrument. I do not mean to discourage the amateur or the student. Quite to the contrary, I want rather to encourage him to study the proper music. It should be everyone's aim and ambition to become master of his instrument, but this can only be done with legitimate and systematic study.

Time and time again, I have seen beginners trying to take up solos which were far beyond their reach. The result of such practice is that their entire progress is retarded . How many hundreds of players attempt to perform the Hartmann and Levy solos, for instances, and how many are really able to do them justice? How many more secure triple-tongue polkas and waste time and energy on them!

My wish in this chapter is simply to advise players not to indulge in the practice of music that is beyond them. There is plenty of music published, and if a little more care were to be exercised in its selection, each player could find numbers that he could master. A simple piece, well played, is certainly better to listen to than a difficult one badly played. Of course, there are many who wish to display technic, even though they do not possess it.

Technic is the only thing that seems to appeal to a large majority. Tonal quality and beautiful phrasing do not appeal to them, when in reality this should be the performer's first aim.

In studying a new solo, first look it over carefully, without playing. Look at the time and tempo marks, the change of keys, marks of expression, repeat signs, etc. Then play it very slowly at first, so that each and every note can be distinctly seen and comprehended. Continue to play slowly, until you are sure of every note, and can play without hesitation. Always bear in mind the old saying: "Any fool can play fast, but it takes a good musician to play slowly." Chopin said: "Every difficulty slurred over will be a ghost to disturb your repose

---

Inasmuch as most good things are produced by labor, it follows that all such things of right belong to those whose labor has produced them.—*Lincoln.*

later on." These are certainly good sayings for the performer
to remember. After having played the solo over in a slow tempo
until you are thoroughly familiar with it, it is then time to begin
to play it faster by degrees. This is the way to secure perfect
control and surety. Most performers when they see a page that
is black with sixteenth and thirty-second notes, immediately
try to play it with the desired amount of speed. The result is
that they never master it, and the hundredth time they make
the same mistakes as the first, and are just as uncertain. Those
whose technic is faultless, are the ones who practice slowly and
with understanding.

Triple tonguing solos should not be attempted until one
has studied and mastered the necessary exercises. Fantasies and
variations can be studied only if the player has the necessary
technic required to perform them. There are many fantasies
that are effective, brilliant and showy, and still not difficult,
and such solos need not necessarily contain any triple tonguing.
The student who is building up a repertoire should not neglect
to study some good songs.

In conclusion, let me say again, do not go beyond your
limit. Make the best of your time and opportunity and do not
waste it on things that are going to do you more harm than
good. Stick to the solos that are within your grasp and try to
advance step by step to the more difficult and advanced forms.

Building a Repertoire: As soon as a player is able to
perform solos, he must start to build a repertoire, and this is a
task that needs careful attention. Every soloist must prepare a
certain number of solos that he will be ready to play at all
times. This does not mean that he must know a hundred solos
that can be played from memory, but every performer should
have at least a dozen or more that have been thoroughly mastered and which can be played without notes at any time.
Many players claim that they have considerable trouble in
memorizing music, and others seem unable to memorize at all.
A person who studies his music carefully should really not have
much trouble committing it to memory, especially if he practices it slowly at first, and analyzes and looks at each and every
note carefully. Too many people try to play by ear instead, or
after playing a piece once or twice, try to perform it from
memory. This is certainly wrong. The music should be played

All the arts, which have a tendency to raise man in the scale of being, have a
certain common bond of union, and are connected, if I may be allowed to say so,
by blood relationship with one another.—*Cicero.*

from notes time and time again, until the performer has formed a mental picture of it. Music should be studied in sections. In a long solo, for instance, it would not be wise to start at the beginning and play to the end each time. Each part should be studied separately, and played over and over again. The soloist who does not play from memory rarely makes a good impression.

In building up a repertoire it is necessary to have solos in different styles. First of all, some songs are essential, and besides high class ones, a few light and catchy ones should be included for encore purposes. Then a few fantasias should be added. There are so many solos of this style published that the performer will be able to include enough to suit all tastes. Polkas have always been popular with soloists and with audiences, and a few of these could be added. In studying a repertoire, the performer must choose solos that he has the ability to perform, first of all, and then he must be sure that they are going to please his listeners.

A repertoire, cannot be worked up all at once. Each solo must be thoroughly mastered before the next is attempted. The numbers of your repertoire must be ready to be played whenever you are called upon to do so. They must be kept in readiness constantly. If a piece is once perfectly memorized, it will never be forgotten. As the repertoire grows your ability to memorize will increase.

A little advice regarding what to play in public will probably be very apropos here. Contrasts should always be sought. For instance, if the number programmed is a song which may be slow and sombre, play as an encore something that will be lively and catchy. If a piece which displays the technic is performed as a first number, use as an encore a song or slow movement that will show your tonal quality and good phrasing. If the first solo is long, the second should always be short. In fact, any encore should *never* be very long.

It must always be borne in mind that without a good and varied repertoire no soloist can expect to have success. Classical, sacred and popular numbers must be included, and then the performer must know just what music will be suitable for each individual occasion. If he knows to what kind of an audience he is to play, he can be sure of creating a vast amount of enthusiasm by selecting numbers that are appropriate. Most

Some neglect the gift that is in them because they are so busy in looking after the gift that is in somebody else.—*C. H. Spurgeon.*

people like the music with which they are familiar, and it is always a good idea in playing encores to render music that the audience knows. A clever soloist can win any audience, providing he has prepared a repertoire which contains music of various kinds.

Players should keep up to date, and not be satisfied to play the same solos which they performed years ago. New music and new ideas should be sought constantly. Good music is always good, whether it be old or new, but if we would keep up to the times and know what is being produced, we must keep posted as to what is being published from time to time.

I do the very best I know how—the very best I can; and I mean to keep doing so until the end. If the end brings me out all right, what is said against me won't amount to anything. If the end brings me out wrong, ten thousands angels swearing that I was right would make no difference.—*Abraham Lincoln.*

CHAPTER XXIX.

CADENZAS

Most instrumental solos in the larger forms contain several cadenzas, as do many of the well-known operatic arias and other vocal numbers. In some instances, these cadenzas have really made the arias famous. Instrumental cadenzas for piano, violin, 'cello, flute, clarinet and cornet appear so frequently that they become a very important item to soloists as well as to those who occupy the first positions in our orchestras and bands. As a general thing cadenzas are difficult, but this is not always the case. Orchestra and band players frequently become alarmed when they are confronted with a piece that contains a cadenza, because the cadenza is always a solo. Soloists, on the contrary, lay a great deal of importance upon these passages, and often when selecting new music will look first at the cadenza to see if it is effective and elaborate enough.

When a cadenza (or cadence) is found, it indicates that the measure of time is suspended, and its performance left to the pleasure and judgement of the player. It should be played tastefully and, as a rule, to correspond with the general character of the composition. There is absolutely no rule for the playing of cadenzas, and it is left entirely to the taste and discretion of the performer. Very often cadenzas are written simply to show the range of the instrument, and the technical capabilities of the performer. In many instances soloists change the cadenzas in order to display their own strong points. They even insert entire new ones at times. Very often the composer leaves it to the performer to use his own cadenzas, so that he can display to the best advantage his capabilities as a performer. It is much easier to render effectively music which has to be played in a certain designated and strict time, such as 4–4, 6–8, 3–4, etc. But in cadenzas, where the regular time is dispensed with, it requires considerable taste and skill to make them sound artistic and impressive. They are often very long, and the more

---

Familiarity does not breed contempt, except of contemptible things, or in contemptible people.—*Phillips Brooks.*

extensive they are the more difficult it becomes to render them so as to hold the attention of the auditors. In playing together with other instruments, many little defects can be concealed, but in the cadenza, which is absolutely free, open and unaccompanied, the performer must rely on a faultless rendition to be successful.

Most players seem to think that every cadenza must be played with the utmost speed. In fact, they seem to imagine that the quicker it is finished the better. All cadenzas are to be played in an "ad libitum" manner, which means that the performer can interpret it according to his own ideas. Freedom and repose are two strong essentials. Ten good cornetists, for instance, would probably play the same cadenza in ten different manners, and each would be correct. Then, again, it is possible for a performer to render the same cadenza in a slightly different manner each time he plays it, and each interpretation may be acceptable. These passages give the player a rare opportunity to display his musicianship, and they also serve to magnify all of his defects, particularly in regard to phrasing.

Mention of some of the cadenzas that are known to all musicians will probably be in place here. One of the best known appears in the Page's Aria from "The Hugenots," by Meyerbeer. This is a very brilliant and elaborate one. Another famous one is to be found in the Polonaise from "Mignon," by Ambroise Thomas. This is a great favorite with singers. As an instrumental solo it is generally played on the clarinet. In the opera "Lucia di Lammermoor" there is a very long cadenza for soprano and flute. Such cadenzas were formerly very popular. All the famous concertos for violin and piano contain cadenzas, and in works of this character these passages are sometimes extremely long, often occupying all of one or two full pages.

In regard to vocal music, cadenzas do not appear very often for the male voices. In the operas of the old school the cadenza was a fixture. In many instances, where the soprano, who generally had the leading role, desired to make more play of her vocal powers, she would request the composer to insert a special cadenza for her. Often such parts were added long after the opera was written, and for different singers the composer would often write different cadenzas. If the contralto happened to be an artist of prominence the composer would sometimes be compelled to add some especially showy music for her, too,

Persistent people begin their success where others end in failure.
—*Edward Eggleston.*

so that she could display her art more prominently. These cadenzas were often the cause of much jealousy and bitter feeling among opera singers. In modern operatic music the cadenza is not used very frequently, but in instrumental music it continues to be a thing of great importance. The student must be impressed with the fact that in order to render a cadenza effectively it must be faultlessly played. Too many performers play solos with cadenzas that are far beyond their capabilities. Cornetists in particular often struggle through cadenzas in a most discouraging manner. It should always be remembered that if the audience can see what a terrible amount of exertion such passages entail, they will not be greatly impressed, and instead of admiring the player for his skill and marvelous control, they will be moved to pity him. The cadenza that is properly mastered will be played with fluency. Many cadenzas in the difficult cornet solos can be performed only by real artists, and the composer often includes a simpler one for other players. This plan is often followed and is to be commended.

Always bear in mind that the cadenza must receive special attention and study. Whatever faults and shortcomings you possess will loom up in magnified form in the playing of the cadenza, whether it be in regard to tone, technique or phrasing.

Remember that there is nothing stable in human affairs; therefore avoid undue elation in prosperity, or undue depression in adversity.—*Isocrates.*

PART IV

CHAPTER XXX.

HOW TO IMPROVE BANDS

It is necessary to raise the standard of bands and band music, and there are many ways in which this can be accomplished. Good results are scarcely possible where there is not a proper balance of instruments. An adequate and proper instrumentation is necessary. Many of our present-day bands go after quantity rather than quality, and there are many bands of from sixty to over a hundred players which are not well balanced. A large number of these bands have entirely too many Saxophones, or perhaps too many Trumpets. They seldom have too many Clarinets, Oboes, Bassoons, Flutes or French Horns. A large band is a very impressive thing—but tonal quality and tonal blending should never be sacrificed for a thoroughly unbalanced mass of sound. Therefore, one way of improving bands is to keep each section supplied with a proportionate allotment of instruments.

In numerous cities and towns of moderate size—there are often six, eight or even ten small professional, semi-professional and amateur bands, all fighting one another. No small town is able to support so many bands, or become interested in or enthusiastic about all of them. It would be far better to merge the better players from each band into one or two completely equipped organizations, and it would then be easier to secure support and recognition, both of which are highly necessary. It is my belief that small bands without a well-balanced instrumentation have prejudiced many a listener against the band. A band of from ten to twenty players cannot possibly give a good account of itself unless it consists of excellent players, and unless the music is specially arranged for its particular combination of instruments. I do not wish to discourage small bands,

---

No men living are more worthy to be trusted than those who toil up from poverty; none less inclined to take or touch aught which they have not honestly earned.
—*Abraham Lincoln.*

for many of our largest and best bands have started in the smallest possible manner. I do say, however, that where there are five, six or more small bands in a city, it would be better to merge them, and try to build up one or two complete bands.

The instruments of percussion are generally sadly neglected. Players are frequently assigned to the percussion because they are unmusical and perhaps unable to learn to play other instruments. This is a great mistake. Musicians realize what a nuisance an inferior bass drummer can be. No one should be considered for this position but a man who has a good musical ear, who has learned the rudiments of music, learned to play some other instrument, and has a keen sense of rhythm. Good bass drummers are tremendously important, and very rare. Most of them have never learned the various ways of striking the drum. The player of the small or snare drum must also have a sense of rhythm. Very few snare drum players can perform a good roll, and many of them cannot read music.

As for the Cymbals, a most important instrument, they, besides helping in the rhythmic effects, add greatly to the climaxes. The Cymbals used in most bands seem to have little or no resonance and ring, sounding more like two tin pans. A really fine pair of Cymbals is an asset to any Band. It is a mistake to allow the bass drum and Cymbals to be manipulated by one man. In order to get the proper effect the Cymbals ought to be beaten with an up-and-down stroke. Players of percussion instruments are frequently put to great expense (if they have to purchase their own instruments) for there seems to be no limit to the many traps they are required to possess. They must have traps to produce every sort of an effect. The players generally are supplied with adequate traps, but the Cymbals seem to be the weak spot in bands. Good Cymbals are rather expensive. Where the player is unable to purchase Cymbals of a fine quality, the band should purchase and own them.   The pair of Cymbals used in my own band is owned by me personally and I value them very highly. They are as carefully guarded as any other instrument in the band.

While on the subject of the Percussion Section, it is quite opportune to say that in many of the older, and even in a few of the newer editions for bands, the arrangement of the drum parts is inexcusably faulty. Many arrangers in transcribing works of such masters as Mozart, Haydn, Handel, Beethoven,

---

Those who deny freedom to others deserve it not for themselves, and under a just God cannot long retain it.—*Abraham Lincoln.*

Mendelssohn, and others, add Bass Drum and Cymbal parts throughout, as though these compositions were military marches, whereas in the original orchestral score there was only a part for the Tympani. Music written without such parts is most assuredly spoiled by the addition of them. A band arrangement should follow the orchestral score closely in this particular. Bandmasters should be careful about this, in playing the music of the masters, Serious bandmasters generally familiarize themselves with the orchestral scores, in the case of classic music. The practice of some arrangers of filling in drum parts where there should be none, has helped to lower the standing of the band in the eyes of many musicians.

A great need of today is that of better arrangers for band. It is a field that offers great opportunity for serious students of bands and band music. Band arrangements in general, have been very stereotyped. Almost each band arranger seems to have a certain style or system to which he adheres. They do not employ the wonderful resources of the many different tonal effects and tonal combinations that are possible. In the olden days the publisher did not permit the arrangers much leeway because they insisted upon having the arrangements simplified and "cued in" so they could be advertised as playable by very large or very small bands with equally good effect. This is not possible. In these days, however, there is a great opportunity for the competent arranger. He can help to raise the band from its slumber of years to new and greater heights. Whether one likes Jazz Bands or not, it must be admitted that most of the better ones owe their success to the fine arrangements which were specially made for them. Some of these arrangements have been truly remarkable. If small Jazz Bands with limited facilities can accomplish this, just think of what the Modern Concert Band will have to offer the world with the advent of some talented arrangers with new and original ideas. We must get away from the stiff, stilted, and routine methods of the past. The band offers a richness of coloring which as yet has not begun to be explored. When arrangers begin to take advantage of their opportunities for original and artistic arrangements, a new era for bands and band music will be at hand.

Touring Bands have not been as plentiful or as successful during the last few years as in the past. Radio is perhaps one of the causes, but there are, of course, other reasons which date

Laziness travels so slowly that poverty soon overtakes him.—*Benjamin Franklin*.

from before the time radio became popular. Bands such as the Sousa organization have reflected great credit upon the profession at large, because of their artistic achievements, as well as their general appearance and demeanor. There have been other touring bands, however, that have reflected no glory upon themselves or anyone else. Some of these bands have made it impossible for worthwhile bands to tour. Many of them have not been worthy of serious consideration as to their performance, and their appearance alone, with their variety of shabby uniforms, doomed them to failure from the start. We have all seen these bands which are anything but uniform in their dress. A good way to make a favorable impression from the very start is to pay strict attention to the appearance of the band, whether it appears in military uniform or civilian clothes. Then the stage deportment is a thing that must be perfect. Absolute attention must be paid to the conductor. There must be strict discipline at all rehearsals and performance, and the conductor must be the "boss."

In order to have a good band we must have good players. Good players must have the very best instruments obtainable. It can be stated without fear of contradiction that the best wind instruments in the world are made in America. Our brass instruments cannot be excelled. In one or two instances there is a tendency to look to Europe for some of the more delicate reed instruments, but in general America leads the world. In many instances European countries are purchasing American-made instruments. We are fortunate in having a number of fine wind instrument makers, and they have done much to stimulate the advancement of bands. A great part of the success of any band depends upon its instruments. Instruments must be well in tune, of good tonal quality, and have perfect mechanism. These are the three prime requisites.

What has been needed in America for many years is a sort of Kneller Hall (the famous Band School of England) in which bandmasters and band players are carefully trained. During the past few years several band schools have been organized here, most of which were short-lived. One or two of them have survived, and it is hoped that these, or at least one of them, will eventually become the Kneller Hall of America. With the

I like to see a man proud of the place in which he lives. I like to see a man live so that his place will be proud of him. Be honest, but hate no one; overturn a man's wrongdoing, but do not overturn him unless it must be done in overturning the wrong. Stand with anybody that stands aright. Stand with him while he is right and help him when he goes wrong.—*Abraham Lincoln.*

tremendous growth of bands there is need for bandmasters who have had a better course of serious training. The progress of many bands is retarded by the inexperience and incompetence of their conductors.

Most conductors pay too little attention to the middle parts—the second, third and fourth parts. They frequently believe that if they have one good cornetist, for example, he will be able to carry all the others along. This is not so. If they have three good cornetists they are generally seated together and play the first part. Second and third parts must be as perfectly played as the first part, and that is what makes the ideal band. The second and third parts always need more rehearsing than the first. In many instances the second and third parts are more difficult to play well. Those who play the melody parts have a slight advantage over the others. It would make for better musicianship and better performers if the conductor would change the players and the parts about occasionally, especially at rehearsals. The players, too, should be made to realize how important the inner or middle parts are. Conductors should always see however, that the melody part predominates slightly over the others but not so as to be obtrusive. Gustav Mahler, one of the world's greatest conductors of the past, once said that when the melody is covered or does not stand out as it should, the music sounds ordinary.

The suggestions made in this chapter, can abet the improvement of bands only if followed in conjunction with suggestions made in more detail throughout the book. Adequate rehearsing, proper music and good editions, and correct usage of instruments (particularly Cornet and Trumpet) are subjects discussed separately. It will suffice here to reiterate that they are factors of primary importance in the improvement of bands.

Never believe all you hear; for he who believes all he hears often will believe that which is not.—*Old Arabian.*

CHAPTER XXXI.

POINTERS FOR BANDSMEN

Watch the conductor closely.

Always remember that the conductor is responsible for the interpretation of the music, so follow his directions whether you approve of them or not.

Make it a point to help the conductor in every possible way.

Come to rehearsal and concerts at least ten or fifteen minutes before starting time.

Look the music over well before playing it.

When the conductor raps for attention, stop whatever you are doing and get ready to play. When he raps the second time put instrument to lips, ready to start.

Assume a position of comfort on the stage, but sit erect. Do not cross your legs.

Be careful of your appearance. Always look neat and have your instrument properly polished.

Never start playing without first having tuned your instrument.

In justice to yourself and the band, learn your part thoroughly. If you cannot play it properly at rehearsal, take it home and study it.

Do not handle the music carelessly. Remember that each part is valuable.

Do not come to rehearsal just to pass the time. Be interested in what you are doing. If a composition has to be repeated many times do not become discouraged. Remember that "Practice Makes Perfect."

Be sure to practice each day. Do not take your instrument up at rehearsals only, and expect to achieve satisfactory results.

Observe all expression marks.

Band players should learn to play softly. As a rule, each performer tries to see how loudly he can play. Remember

---

Do not say all you know; for he who says all he knows often will say that which he knows not.—*Old Arabian.*

there must be contrast. Playing loudly continually will eventually ruin one's playing.

Rehearsals should not last longer than two hours, and there should be an intermission after the first hour or so.

Do precisely as the leader suggests. If you think you know more than he does, do not let him know it.

If you play a first part in the band do not look down upon the other players; they are just as important as you are.

Do not imagine that you cannot be replaced. The world will go on just the same if someone else, who may not play quite so well as you, is required to fill your position.

Be fair in your criticisms and do not condemn everyone who doesn't think as you do.

Respect others for their achievements, knowledge, and experience. Try to learn from your superiors.

In regard to an instrument, secure the best one you can, for the best is always the cheapest in the long run.

All band players should strive to become good sight readers. This will help any organization to make rapid progress.

Take an active and personal interest in your organization. Do not let others do all the work.

Do not think that as soon as you become a member of a band you require no further study. Continue to study and take lessons as long as you can.

Play with as little effort as possible.

See that your position is good whether sitting or standing. Appearance is important.

Wind instrument players should tune their instruments frequently during the course of playing; cold and heat affect the intonation. Cold makes instruments flat, and heat sharpens them.

Do not think that tuning once with other instruments will suffice for the entire season. The lips are not always in the same condition, and consequently the intonation will not always be the same.

Be careful what you eat, and keep your stomach in good condition. If the stomach is not right, the lips will suffer. Blisters on the lips, fever sores, and dryness come either from stomach disorders or a cold. Do not allow yourself to become

---

Errors like Straw
Upon the surface flow,
He who would search for pearls
Must dive below.
                              —*Dryden.*

constipated. Do not eat much before playing. One should never play directly after eating a heavy meal. Allow the food to digest.

Do not drink much liquor, and smoke only in moderation if at all. Too much smoking makes one short winded and makes the lips and tongue dry. Too much liquor affects the tongue very materially.

Do not mark time with your feet while playing. This is a serious fault. The player who indulges in this is taking his own tempo rather than that which the conductor is desginating. Conductors must insist that all performers keep their feet still while playing, otherwise good rhythmic results will be impossible.

Tobacco chewing is a bad habit for wind players to acquire.

Do not neglect the teeth. They are essential to the proper playing of any wind instrument. Teeth should be brushed on rising in the morning and after each meal if possible, but particularly before retiring at night. Particles of food cling to the teeth after eating and are apt to be blown into the instrument.

Wind instrument players require plenty of sleep and as much fresh air as possible. Eight hours sleep is a good average. Take long walks daily if possible and fill the lungs with fresh air.

Sleep with your bedroom windows wide open summer and winter. Fresh air will never hurt anyone.

Do not think that you are beyond the point of learning more and more. One is never too old to learn.

Practice regularly every day. Three or four hours one day and nothing the next day or two cannot bring good results. It is better to practice a shorter time each day, and do it with regularity.

Go to your practice as though it were pleasure and not torture.

Remember that every exercise has some definite purpose in view. If you do not know the object of the exercise, you do not get the benefit of it.

Practice each exercise until you have mastered it.

Beginners should practice only about twenty minutes at a time, two or three times a day.

Advanced players would do well to practice one-half hour at a time, three, four, or five times a day.

It is a poor heart, and a poorer age, that cannot accept the conditions of life with some heroic readiness.—*Stevenson.*

The player who knows how and what to practice will accomplish more in half an hour than the person who practices aimlessly three or four hours a day.

Do not play for an hour or two at a time and tire the lips.

Cease practicing before the lips tire.

Practice what you are deficient in.

Remember that many exercises which seem monotonous and uninteresting are often the most beneficial.

Do not confine your practice solely to exercises of one sort.

Do not waste time practicing things that are of no value.

The most difficult exercises and solos are comparatively easy if you approach them in a systematic and progressive manner.

Good results cannot possibly be achieved if, after having a few lessons, one expects to play the most difficult music. Without some definite system not much progress can be made.

There is a reason for every fault. If you know the fault, find the reason, and remedy it.

Do not get into the habit of practicing with a mute. Practice sustained tones before anything else each day. Play them softly.

The person who can play most loudly has not the best embouchure. Anyone can play loudly. The person who can play softly and smoothly, and modulate his tones, has good lip control. The player who can play only loudly may be a good noise maker, but not a good musician.

Play before a mirror when practicing so that you can see how you look. The mirror is truthful, so look into it often.

It is better to stand when practicing, as it gives more freedom.

Avoid the tremolo. Let your tones be steady and clear.

Do not press the mouthpiece too tightly against the lips. Do not expect the lips to become hard like a piece of wood. It is not necessary to raise a "corn" on the lips. The lips remain soft and pliable, but the muscles become developed.

Do not practice high tones exclusively.

The notes of the middle and lower registers should be practiced daily. Acquire the high tones by degrees. It takes considerable time to get them under perfect control. Overdoing of the high tones tends to weaken the lips.

The prime condition for discovering the truth is to be free from all prejudice.
—*Renan.*

Do not attempt double or triple tonguing until you can single tongue perfectly.

Every form of playing should be taken up at the proper time.

Hear all the good music you can. Imitate the style of the artists whether they be singers or instrumentalists.

Indulge in ensemble practice whenever possible.

Playing with others helps develop the ear.

Knowing the words of songs will help towards giving a better rendition on your instrument.

Do not boast or try to lead-others to believe that you are something you are not.

There is no such thing as perfection and nothing is so good that it cannot be better.

Encourage those who know less than you.

If it is possible to get a teacher, do not indulge in self-instruction. Self-instruction is only advisable when it is not possible to secure a competent teacher.

You do not hear or see your own faults. A good teacher will detect your faults and thus they may be remedied. With proper instruction progress should be rapid and complete.

Remember, the teacher can only correct, guide and advise you. If you do not follow the teacher's instructions, you are wasting time and money.

Respect your teacher and have full confidence in him, otherwise nothing can be accomplished.

Ask questions. This shows that you are thinking, and anxious to be set right on points about which you are in doubt.

In practicing your exercises, remember the corrections the the teacher makes. Always go to your teacher with lessons well prepared.

A little progress should be made with each succeeding lesson. The pupil does not always know whether or not he is progressing because he constantly hears himself play.

Be sure to keep your instrument clean, particularly the inside. Brass players should run water through their instruments once a week or even every day, if possible.

Remember, there is no such thing as a perfect wind instrument. To play well, in tune, one must have a good lip and keen ear.

Ear training is necessary for every wind instrument player.

This is the bitterest of all—to wear the yoke of our wrong-doing.—*George Eliot.*

Do not condemn instruments if you do not know how to tune them.

It is not possible to have the lips in the same condition every day. Even the greatest players have good and bad days.

Become familiar with the music of the masters. Study the history of music.

Never be without a musical dictionary.

Genius is supposed to be a power of producing excellencies which are out of the reach of the rules of art; a power which no precepts can teach, and which no industry can acquire.—*Sir Joshua Reynolds.*

CHAPTER XXXII.

IMPORTANT SUGGESTIONS FOR WIND INSTRUMENT PLAYERS.

I. FOR DEVELOPING TONE

Play sustained tones each day before attempting anything else. This must be done with great regularity.

Devote from 15 to 30 minutes to this sort of practice each day.

First play the notes in the medium register of the instrument, then the lower tones and, lastly, the higher ones.

Hold each note for about 8 slow counts.

Do not make any crescendos or descrescendos on the tones, but keep them perfectly steady. The crescendo and descrescendo are very beneficial in practice, but they should not be attempted until one has acquired absolute steadiness of tone and a certain amount of control.

Rest for about 4 counts between the notes. This gives time for exhaling and inhaling and allows one to play with more freedom and ease. At the same time it gives the muscles of the lips an opportunity to relax.

Do not tire the lips. Rest frequently during practice time.

After playing the notes of the medium register begin the notes of the lower register. Go back and forth in this register for 5 or 10 minutes.

After a rest start the tones from the middle register, going as high as you can with perfect ease.

Do not force the tones. If the higher tones do not respond with ease do not force them, but descend again.

For higher tones do not use much pressure, but contract the muscles, particularly those at the corners of the mouth.

With the proper kind of patience and systematic practice, the high tones will eventually begin to respond with ease.

Above all, have patience and do not imagine that a good, sure and reliable embouchure is to be acquired in a few months.

Everyone is the son of his own work.—*Cervantes.*

For the lower tones, the muscles must be most relaxed.

In this kind of daily practice, the long tones should not be over-blown. The greatest benefit will be derived if they are played about mezzo forte.

The tone need not be attacked forcefully, but rather with clarity and precision.

It must be remembered that the breath is the life of the tone and therefore it must be sustained with evenness.

After the long tones have been gone over, it would be wise to lay the instrument aside for at least 10 or 15 minutes for rest.

After that, other exercises in various forms should be practiced.

It must be borne in mind that the practice of sustained tones is the only form of practice that will improve one's tonal quality, strengthen the lips and give one the necessary endurance and power.

The playing of songs and sustained melodies should be indulged in to some extent each day. This should be done after the various exercises have been completed.

The daily playing of long tones is not only for the beginner or amateur, but should be indulged in with the strictest regularity by the advanced player as well.

Nothing will keep the lips in such condition as this form of practice.

II. FOR DEVELOPING THE TONGUE.

Without accurate tonguing, it will be absolutely impossible to become a good performer on any wind instrument.

The tonguing of most players seems heavy and indistinct.

Tonguing is another form that must be practiced daily.

Almost every method contains suitable exercises. The trouble is that so few practice them properly.

One can hardly secure a good tone without tonguing properly, therefore if one is able to produce the sustained tones properly he should, with proper practice, be able to train his tongue in the right direction.

Most people have trouble in tonguing rapidly and are unable to get the tongue and fingers to act simultaneously.

The tongue should not protrude beyond the lips. This would cause the lips to move each time the tongue moves, with

---

Few persons have courage enough to appear as good as they really are.
—*A. W. Hare.*

the result that there could not possibly be any pressure or steadiness.

The lips should not move. The tongue must move from the inside.

The tongue should not move much. The smaller distance it moves the sharper the tonguing will be and the more rapid.

Many players move their lips with every note they strike because the tongue protrudes too far.

It is a serious mistake to practice all exercises rapidly because they happen to be written in 16th and 32nd notes. Such notes denote speed, but in practice they should be played very slowly at first. As one acquires control of the exercise they can be played quicker. Never attempt to play quicker than your technique warrants. Remember the old saying: "Any fool can play fast, but it takes a good musician to play slowly."

III. PERTAINING TO MOUTHPIECES.

The mouthpiece is such an important part of the instrument that it is blamed for almost all defects in one's playing. Very often this blame is properly placed, but not in most cases.

It is a difficult matter indeed to decide which particular mouthpiece is best suited to a beginner. In fact, there is no possible way of choosing a certain mouthpiece and insisting that it is the one he must use. Only one who has acquired an embouchure and has the proper and sensitive feeling in his lips can judge a mouthpiece—and what suits one may not suit another.

The beginner should be started with the regulation mouthpiece of legitimate size. After he is able to play a little his teacher should be able to decide whether the mouthpiece suits or not. If it does not, other mouthpieces can be tried. When one is finally decided upon, the student will probably be able to use it as long as he lives.

Many professionals as well as amateur players change their mouthpieces constantly. This is a serious mistake indeed, one that will do more harm than good in the end.

It will be easier to get the high notes on one than on another, just as it will be easier to play low tones on one than on another. Some will produce a larger tone—others a smaller one.

A good reader summons the mighty dead from their tombs and makes them speak.—*Emerson.*

After the proper mouthpiece is found it does not mean that you will immediately have perfect control of your instrument. It does not mean that the high notes will come of themselves, or that you will have unlimited power and endurance.

The development of the lips is far more important than the mouthpiece.

Remember that if the lips are properly developed you can get some kind of a result on almost any mouthpiece, but without the lip control there is not a mouthpiece in the world that will help.

IV. PLAYERS OF BRASS INSTRUMENTS

For players of Brass Instruments the following will be most important:

The mouthpiece of medium proportion—not too deep or too shallow—will give the best result.

Some players use a mouthpiece with too deep a cup—others with too shallow a cup. The shape and depth of the cup have a decided effect upon the tonal quality. The size of the rim also—its curvature or flatness—is an important item.

The mouthpiece must feel comfortable on the lips by all means. The edges must not cut in.

It is wrong to use a trumpet mouthpiece on a cornet, or a cornet mouthpiece on a trumpet.

A trumpet mouthpiece has a shallower cup and a long stem which helps to give a thinner and sharper tone. The cornet mouthpiece is deeper and has a shorter stem. The result is a broader tone. Each must be used in its proper place to give the desired effect.

For those who are compelled to play on the cornet and the trumpet, it would be wise for them to see that the rims of both mouthpieces are precisely the same and the cups different. There are many so-called "combination mouthpieces" on the market today which answer the purpose very well. They are made with a screw rim which can be screwed onto the cornet cup or the trumpet cup.

When you have found the proper mouthpiece stick to it. Do not blame the poor mouthpiece for all your shortcomings. Remember that without an embouchure no mouthpiece in the world will serve you properly.

The path of democracy is education.—*E. H. Griggs.*

For reasons of sanitation never allow anyone to use your mouthpiece.

Always see that the mouthpiece is absolutely clean inside and out.

A country is false to itself if it does not keep in view the good of all mankind.
—*Sir Oliver Lodge.*

CHAPTER XXXIII.

THE PLAYING OF TWO INSTRUMENTS

Is it necessary or advisable for a person to play two different instruments? This is a frequent query and one that can be discussed from several viewpoints. It is not, of course, necessary to play two instruments, but it most assuredly is advisable for a person who has gained proficiency on one instrument to take up another, if only to get a working knowledge of it.

To master any one instrument, properly, requires years of constant study and practice, and it would, therefore, be ridiculous to suggest that the student start studying two instruments at the same time. Most people have all they can do to acquire proficiency on one. Others, again, have a natural gift for the study of music and for instruments in particular, and to them there seem to be no insurmountable difficulties. Naturally, we prefer to hear a person who plays only one instrument well, than a performer who plays several poorly. In most instances, the player who endeavors to study two or three instruments at the same time, devoting the same amount of time to each, fails. He may become a fair performer, but he usually is not a *great* success on any of the instruments.

In almost every large symphony orchestra, men will be found who are capable performers on two or more instruments. They may be fine musicians and extremely talented. Few of these men, however, play the first or important parts, because of the fact that they devoted too much time to the study of several instruments and too little detailed attention to any one in particular. On the other hand, most of the leading orchestra players are men who devoted most of their time to one special instrument, and while the majority of them can play two, the second was only taken up after the first was mastered, and as an accomplishment.

These assertions apply only in a general way, and many

Good counsels observed, are claims to grace; neglected, are halters to strange, undutiful children.—*T. Fuller.*

exceptions can be cited. As an example, we might mention Fritz Kreisler, who besides being one of the world's greatest violinists, is also an excellent pianist. Marcella Sembrich, the famous opera singer, appeared first as a violinist and pianist. Both Kreisler and Sembrich are artists of world-wide repute and both are musical geniuses. Their whole lives have been devoted to music and while both had to struggle for success in their earlier careers, they were naturally able to master and overcome the difficulties of their instruments more readily than most players, because of their remarkable talents and gifts. There are numerous other examples of famous players who are proficient on two instruments. It will be noticed, however, that their reputations were acquired through their mastery of one instrument, the one to which they were more attracted and to which they devoted most of their energies.

The playing of one instrument is often a great help in acquiring command of another, but in some instances it is a great and serious drawback. Most violinists find very little difficulty in learning to play the piano, at least well enough for their own amusement, or for some practical purpose. The violinist who is able to play a piano accompaniment part will derive benefit in many ways. It will enable him to study and learn his solos in a musical and scholarly manner, and he will be able to accompany others—particularly his pupils. As a matter of fact, every person who takes up the study of a stringed or wind instrument should learn to play the piano. Nothing is more important. Piano playing will give one an insight into almost everything pertaining to music; harmony, form, counterpoint, and the opportunity to study the entire literature of music and to become familiar with it, whether it be symphonic, operatic or vocal. The orchestral instruments do not afford or invite this opportunity. The piano may then be said to be the most important instrument as a second choice of every musician. This is, of course, considered purely from a musical standpoint. But there are other viewpoints to be considered.

The orchestral musician who takes up a second instrument chooses one that will, in his opinion, help increase his income. In symphonic and operatic music, there are certain instruments, such as the contra-bassoon, bass-clarinet and bass-trumpet which are only used now and then, to create special effects.

God grants liberty only to those who love it, and are always ready to guard and defend it.—*Daniel Webster.*

These parts are generally played by violin or viola players in the orchestra. Often, too, the score may call for a third clarinet, a third or fourth flute, third or fourth trumpet, fourth trombone, etc. Invariably one of the string players is able to play such parts, and is engaged especially because of the fact that he can be used to double advantage. It is possible for a man to play violin and clarinet, violin and cornet, and so on, but can a person play cornet and French horn, cornet and trombone, or cornet and tuba?

It is almost an impossibility to become an artist on any two different wind instruments. It requires years of constant study and practice on an instrument before an embouchure is acquired, and the study of another is almost bound to prove a disturbing factor. Anyone who plays a cornet realizes that after he has an embouchure it is almost impossible to produce a tone if the mouthpiece is shifted a small fraction of an inch to one side or another. He also knows that if he takes a mouthpiece which differs ever so slightly from the one to which he is accustomed, he will lack surety. Each brass instrument player becomes accustomed to a certain position and place for his mouthpiece and the mouthpiece goes there almost naturally. It rests on certain muscles which develop and become responsive. The person who tries to play cornet and French horn, cornet and trombone, cornet and tuba, cannot possibly achieve fine results on both. He will be able to play the two instruments only after a certain fashion.

There are many bandmasters and band teachers who are possessed of great versatility and who understand each and every band instrument thoroughly; many of them can play all or nearly all of them. In such bands the instructor is generally compelled to teach each instrument because most of the players do not receive or take any other private instruction. It is fortunate for this bandmaster that he can play the various instruments or he would never be able to demonstrate certain points and passages. All honor is due such gifted men. They are for the most part intelligent musicians, who devote their time exclusively to teaching bands, or directing, and do not have to rely upon the playing of any one certain instrument as a means of making a livelihood. If we were to ask them whether it is advisable to study two wind instruments and whether great

---

Kindness has converted more sinners than either zeal, eloquence or learning.
—*F. W. Faber.*

success can be attained on both, they would unquestionably reply, "No." Here, again, there are a few exceptions which no rule seems to escape. A flutist can, and in most cases should also play piccolo. The oboe player may play English horn, the clarinetist may play bass-clarinet, or saxophone. Cornetists can play trumpet, because the two instruments are the same in pitch, and the rim of the mouthpiece is the same. Trombonists can play baritone, or vice versa, because practically the same mouthpiece can be used. But as for a wind instrument player taking up another reed or brass instrument, it is not advisable. To those of the wind instrument players who feel inclined to take up some other medium, none can be more beneficial than the piano or organ, or else one of the stringed instruments, violin, viola, 'cello, or bass. Contrast is what makes the study of any two instruments interesting: therefore, it would seem that string players should seek some wind instrument as a second choice, and wind players, one of the stringed instruments. In both such instances, the results will be beneficial in numerous ways. It should be borne in mind, however, that it is not really a necessity for either the professional or amateur to play two instruments. It is advisable only for those who become proficient on one, and would find it no strain to adopt another— who seek a further outlet for their energy, and desire to open up new spheres of activity.

The worth of art appears most eminent in music, since it requires no material, no subject matter, whose effect must be deducted; it is wholly form and power, and it raises and ennobles whatever it expresses.—*Goethe.*

CHAPTER XXXIV.

NERVOUSNESS AND HOW TO OVERCOME IT.

Nervousness is the cause of more failures among players than any other one thing. Though "players may come and players may go" nervousness "goes on forever." And why should this be? Because it is true that in many cases, the study of years, the preparation of months is brought to naught by this bogy of "nerves." What causes nervousness? We all know its symptons; the icy hands and feet—the numb, gone feeling "somewhere within"—the quickly beating heart—the hot flashes to the head—the dry tongue and lips—the quaking knees—the all-pervading wish to "go through the floor", or any place!

To begin with, nervousness may be due only to lack of familiarity with the work in hand—insufficient surety of one's music, or one's own powers. In this case, the fault lies with the player, and is not difficult to overcome. How can a player expect to get through creditably, if he has not drilled himself to perfection in every detail of his work? How can he go before an audience with his preparation half complete—and feeling not at all sure? He deserves all the pangs of nervousness. But let him study and practice thoroughly every bit of the work in hand—let him be fully prepared, thoroughly familiar, and letter perfect—and he need not be nervous.

Then there is the man who, though fully prepared, letter perfect in his work, yet is afraid! Afraid of himself—afraid he cannot trust himself—tortured and bewildered by doubts and fears that are unnecessary. He has no confidence in himself— he is frightened to death at the thought of an audience. He is over-sensitive—he fears criticism. To him, every whisper, every remark must surely be an adverse criticism. How can such a player get through a performance with any credit to himself? In fact—how can he be anything but a wreck, and his performance

---

If we look around in modern music we will find that we have a terrible deal of mind and astonishingly few ideas.—*Ambros*.

a flat failure? The answer is this. A man suffering from such lack of courage must submit himself to the most rigorous tests to harden his sensitive soul. He must get an audience at any cost—every time he plays. He must school himself to all kinds of harsh criticism and learn to discount it—to ignore it, after he takes out of it what he can get. He must devote his entire attention with every fibre of his being, to the work in hand, with but the single purpose of getting it done, and getting it done as well as it should be done. He must get the approval of those who know—for the best cure for this unhappy creature who really is capable and proficient, but who doubts himself, is the approbation, the approval, whole-hearted and sincere of course, of people who know that he knows.

Contrasted to the man who needs "patting on the back," encouragement to do his splendid "best"—is the man whose nervousness proceeds from over-surety. He is nervous because he may not be appreciated as much as he thinks he should be. He is so certain that he is "all right" that for very cocksureness he becomes nervous. He cannot wait for his turn, he fidgets from one foot to another, bites his nails, and works himself up generally. This man needs to be shown that he is not the only player in the world, possibly not the only performer on the program. He must concede that there are others, and possess his soul in patience. If he is a capable performer, he must not be over-anxious to show what he can do, as he may in truth over-reach himself and spoil his performance.

Outside of these very controllable, and more or less natural causes of nervousness, there are many causes which are not so natural, and yet are in a great measure as easily controlled. The first of these is poor health. This is, of course, a large subject, and one on which volumes might be written. We can touch upon it but very lightly, and only in places which bear directly upon the subject under discussion. A man who is suffering from a definite disease can scarcely be expected to acquit himself as creditably as a man in perfect health. And, of course, the comment on this is too obvious to need setting down. However, the secondary causes of poor health, aside from actual illness and disease, can readily be met with and discussed.

Under this heading there is, first and foremost as a cause of nervousness, insufficient, irregular and disturbed sleep. Nothing makes a person feel worse than a "bad night." And a

The artist never seeks to represent the positive truth, but the idealized image of the truth.—*Bulwer*.

player can scarcely have a worse preliminary to a performance than improper sleep. A man who depends upon his playing for his living, especially one who does much solo work, should see to it that his hours are regular. This applies particularly to hours for sleeping. Hours for eating, exercise, recreation and practice should be just as carefully planned, for all these things are absolutely essential to the man who would have his nerves steady at critical moments. He must avoid over-exertion, overwork— too lengthy stretches of time at any one thing. All of these things are prolific producers of nervousness.

In addition to the proper regulation of one's life and mode of living, it is, of course, essential that a player make his life work the subject of constant attention. The acquisition of sufficient concentration to enable one rigidly to exclude everything but the subject in hand is in itself an art not quickly or readily attained. But when one has the power of concentration, and the ability to apply it, the perfection of one's art is made comparatively easy. This, after all, is the keynote of the whole situation. Discounting actual illness or infirmity, nine-tenths of the nervousness among players can be overcome and done away with by these two things—absolute mastery of one's work, and ability to concentrate to the point of excluding everything but one's work.

Art and composition tolerate no conventional fetters; mind and soul soar above them.—*Joseph Haydn.*

CHAPTER XXXV.

THE CARE OF BRASS INSTRUMENTS

It is no exaggeration to say that more instruments are ruined by not being kept clean, than from real wear and tear. Real usage will never hurt an instrument provided it is kept clean. The instrument whose exterior is dirty is bad enough to look at, but if the interior is unclean, the tone and intonation are impaired, as well as the ease of blowing. Worse still—the instrument gives forth a vile and unhealthy odor, and becomes a breeding place for germs of every description.

It must be remembered that the inside of the tubing becomes covered with a slimy coating of saliva, which, if allowed to stand, turns hard, forming deposits of verdigris. This verdigris gets into all remote corners and clogs them up, and besides preventing the bore from being perfectly clear and free, will eventually eat into the metal.

Particles of food are often blown into the instrument, and find lodging in various parts. It is therefore important that the performer cleanse his teeth and rinse his mouth immediately after eating. Dust from the air also collects quickly and settles in the moist inside of instruments.

Cleanliness is economy, and therefore should be indulged in regularly and religiously. It is a good idea to let water run through a brass instrument daily, as that will carry off the slime before it has a chance to harden, and will prevent any obnoxious odors. Once a week a thorough cleansing with hot soapsuds made from good soap can be used. Pour the soapsuds into the bell of the instrument, turning it completely around many times so that every corner is reached; then pour clean water through, holding the valves down, and allow the water to pass through all parts.

If the instrument has been neglected for a while, and becomes clogged with dirt, dissolve a little borax or washing soda in lukewarm water, and pour it into the instrument, allowing it

There are many minds that only work effectively when they do so under compulsion.—*Schumann.*

to remain for a short while. Upon rinsing, it will be surprising to see how much filth has accumulated.

If these methods do not cleanse satisfactorily, the instrument should be sent to a repair shop.

It creates a good impression to see an instrument that is clean and bright externally, too. Plated instruments are easier to keep clean than brass ones, although they do not necessarily give forth better tones. There are many good cleaning preparations on the market.

The valves must be kept immaculately clean if one desires to render any music properly. They should be removed frequently and wiped off with a piece of soft cloth. The openings should also be cleaned thoroughly. The bottom caps should then be removed and the inner valve casings cleaned from top to bottom. Most people use saliva on the valves but the habit of spitting is not to be encouraged. Water will answer the purpose satisfactorily if the valves are kept in good condition. If oil is used it should be an oil that is especially prepared for the purpose, and it must be thin.

In case the valves work sluggishly, cleanse them with kerosene—also the valve casings. Then replace them and work them up and down. After that, wipe off the kerosene and wet the valve with water or fine oil.

Be careful not to bend or strain the valves.

When instruments are not to be used for a long time, remove all valves and slides, and wipe them perfectly dry. This will prevent rust and corrosion.

If the valves are properly fitted and kept in good condition, they should be noiseless. Noise is sometimes caused by the spring rubbing against the stem which it surrounds, or by coming in contact with the chamber in which it is encased. This noise can often be dispensed with by setting the spring properly, or by putting a drop of oil at the point of friction. If the padding or corks are worn out there is also apt to be a noise.

The top and bottom valve caps should be removed often. A drop of oil rubbed around the threading every once in a while will keep them free so that they can be removed at will.

Valve slides should be moved in and out daily so that they do not stick. They should be wiped off at least once a week:

He is a good musician who understands the music without the score and the score without the music.—*Schumann*.

then a very thin coating of fine oil or vaseline applied. This will help keep the slides air tight, and prevent them from sticking. If the slides are rusty, it is advisable to send the instrument to a reliable repair shop.

The cork on the water-key must be replaced as soon as it wears out, and the spring should be oiled every once in a while. The spring should not be too loose or too tight, so that it closes perfectly.

Persons who have a great deal of acid in their systems, and whose hands perspire freely, will generally notice that wherever they hold the instrument the plating is eaten away. Unless they desire to have their instrument plated frequently, it is advisable to wear a glove on the left hand.

Dents spoil the appearance of an instrument, and disturb the air column. They should be removed as soon as possible.

The valves should be air-tight. If after a while they become worn through constant friction, they can be plated and ground in again. Any leak around the valves, slides or water-key will mar the tone, and render the instrument hard blowing.

Slide Trombones require very careful attention. Slides must be removed and cleansed very often.

After playing, remove the water from all parts of the instrument. This is very important. Remove the mouthpiece also.

To me it seems the best thing quietly to proceed on our own road, and, particularly, to beware of a daily evil that does much harm—namely, the habit of squandering and wasting our strength on outward things.—*Felix Mendelssohn.*

CHAPTER XXXVI.

THE CARE OF REED INSTRUMENTS

It is necessary to oil a new instrument, or one that has not been in use for some time, before attempting to play upon it. New instruments require special attention and should be oiled with the finest quality of oil. The oil should not be permitted to soak into the pads.

After an instrument has been in use, and before putting it aside, wipe away all the moisture that has gathered on the interior, and also any accumulation around the cork joints.

Keep the instrument in as even a temperature as possible. Avoid exposing it to very sudden changes of temperature. It must be borne in mind that heat expands and cold contracts.

In the event that the wood of the instrument should swell so that difficulty is experienced in taking it apart, do not use unnecessary force, as this may split the wood.

The joints should be so accurately adjusted that they fit into one another quite easily. The corks alone should hold the joints properly.

The delicate parts of an instrument and the bearings cannot function perfectly forever, without occasional attention. Oil should be applied frequently. Besides acting as a lubricant, and a possible preventative against the cracking of the wood, a little oil occasionally will preserve and improve the mechanism.

Art! who can say that he fathoms it? Who is there capable of discussing the nature of this great goddess?—*Beethoven*.

CHAPTER XXXVII.

CRITICISM

Every person who is in the public eye subjects himself to criticism. It matters not whether he be a musician, painter, sculptor, actor, minister, or public official; whatever he does or says is open to criticism, and in fact, he invites it. The person who cannot stand criticism will not be a success, because criticism irritates and annoys him to such a degree, that after a time he becomes nervous and unable to do himself justice. While in some instances, criticism stimulates one to higher achievements, it has the opposite effect on others, often discouraging them to such an extent that they give up in despair. There are, of course, various kinds and classes of critics, just as there are different sorts of criticism. We are all critics, more or less in all things, whether it pertains to music or not. It seems to be a natural tendency on the part of most people to pick out the weak spots and flaws in everything, and we seem to fail to realize that many of the things criticised have their good points, which often far outnumber the flaws. Almost everything has some redeeming feature, and in passing judgment we ought always try to find some good. As a general thing we express our opinions on subjects about which we know little or nothing, and it is this kind of criticism that is unjust and damaging. If a certain thing does not appeal to us personally we generally condemn it, whereas others may find untold beauties in it. We should consider it from all sides. Unjust criticism has been the ruination of many an artist.

All musicians must realize that whenever and wherever they play they are going to be criticised. If it is a public concert, the professional critic will pass judgment in the daily papers. In a private or social gathering, each person forms his own opinion regarding the performance. The public is guided to a great extent by what the newspaper critics have to say regarding the ability of a performer, and it is often within the

Music is not essentially aristocratic; it is universal, therefore essentially democratic.—*Anonymous.*

power of the critic to "make or break" one. The critic who is capable and fair will point out the strong as well as the weak points in the soloist's playing and will give encouragement where it is deserved. The sensible performer will profit by criticism if he accepts it at its true worth. He must consider each criticism carefully. If defects in his playing are pointed out, he must know or find out from some authority, whether they really exist, and if they do, he must exert every possible effort to overcome them. By heeding such criticism the performer can only profit. Unfortunately, all critics are not actually capable of judging the merits or demerits of one's performance, and the soloist's playing is not always correctly reported. The inferior player often receives more praise than the superior one. Of course, the player does not always do himself justice either, and often when he is anxious to do his best, he is seen at his worst. A violinist may happen to have a poor string, or the weather may affect his instrument. The cornetist may not have a good embouchure, for which he cannot account, and consequently his playing suffers. Every player has good and bad days.

It is, of course, true that a great deal more is expected of players today than was a generation ago, especially as the public has become more educated musically, and there are more artists, and more people who are interested in music. In almost every family someone plays. There are more concerts than ever and almost everybody is interested in some branch of music. Almost every large city, and many of the smaller ones, provide free concerts for the people. The phonograph and radio have also been great factors in bringing a better class of music into the home. Music, therefore, is almost a general topic of conversation these days, and again for this reason performers are subjected to more criticism than ever before.

The modest, ambitious, sensible player will profit through just criticism. On the other hand the conceited, self-satisfied one considers himself beyond criticism, and believes only the good things that are said of him. Whatever is not good, he considers unjust. Unjust criticism can be good or bad. It is just as unfair to call good playing bad, as it is to call bad playing good. There are too many players who really believe that their performance is above criticism. They take the word of none but

---

Mannerism is displeasing in the original, to say nothing of the same fault in copyists.—*Schumann.*

their flattering friends. This flattery has been the greatest drawback to many who might otherwise have achieved great success. Many a head has been turned by undue praise. This is the case principally with young and talented players. Many people praise because they are not able to judge, or detect the weak points. Others flatter, just in order to say something nice, or because they fear to express their true feelings. At best, the subject is one that must be handled with the utmost delicacy.

We go to theatres and to concerts and then discuss the performances with our friends. One person will find a rendition superb, and another will pick it to pieces. Our tastes and ideas are not all alike. The newspaper critics report and analyze the performances of such violinists as Kreisler, Elman, Zimbalist, Heifetz, or pianists like Paderewski, Hofmann, Godowsky, and so on. It would seem almost impossible to find anything to criticise in the playing of such masters; but after hearing them all, the critic finds much to write about, because he learns that each one has one or more particular qualities that makes his playing so wonderful. Each may excel in a different style. He soon learns that they are human too, and that while their playing can never be bad, it is not always on the same high level. These artists expect to be criticized.

Musicians criticise each other almost habitually, and envy very often plays a large part in this. One player will find everything bad that another does. One teacher scorns the success of another, and so on. Criticism in such instances lowers itself to "knocking"—pure and simple. As a rule, it is the musicians who have the poorest schooling, and the most inferior players, who resort to this sort of criticism and knocking. Nothing seems good to them, except what they do themselves. They suffer from an exaggerated "ego" and cannot find a good word for anyone else. They seem to forget that even a player who is not first class, may have some redeeming features. On the contrary, the most lenient critic is generally the one who himself is highly accomplished. The greater the man, it often seems, the simpler and more generous he is. The artist realizes the difficulties in any performance, and makes allowance for the shortcomings. He encourages the talented, and does not criticise harshly. He realizes what years of study one must go through before becoming an artist.

Dare talent permit itself to take the same liberties as genius? Yes; but the former will perish where the latter triumphs.—*Schumann.*

In conclusion, let us hope for fairer and more generous criticisms, especially one performer's criticism of another. Every one who plays must be prepared to stand criticism. He should, therefore, get whatever good he can out of just criticism, and be inspired by it to greater things.

There are untalented people who have been attracted by and hold to music from the force of outward circumstances, and who have learned a great deal—music mechanics.—*Schumann.*

CHAPTER XXXVIII.

ENVY AMONG MUSICIANS

The old saying has it that "Music hath charms to soothe the savage breast," and surely it is the truth. Music affects both the performer and the auditor in some strange, subtle manner of which we are all aware. Under its spell oft-times a great sorrow is forgotten, and under its influence we forget, too, the petty annoyances, the small troubles and the trivialities which frequently are our daily portion.

But away from the music's magic, does the musician forget his little feuds, his quick uprisings of jealousy and of envy? We are all, unfortunately, prone to envy, whether consciously or unconsciously. We wish constantly for what we have not—for what we would like to have—for what our neighbor has. We are none of us satisfied, rarely even the best of us. Perhaps some of the strongest of us, in the buffetings and the living of life, have learned to control our feelings, to refrain from judging —to withhold the expression of our sentiments. But what of the "temperamental" man, the man who cannot or does not (more likely) inhabit his speech or temper his criticism?

The art of criticism is a great art. Without it there would be no standards. But how many are really qualified to criticise? Yet there are not many who do not criticise—and this kind of criticism is usually unfavorable. It is the product of envy. Somehow, to some people, or perhaps I should say, to certain types of people, nothing that others say or do is worth consideration, save for adverse comments. Have we not all competitors in every field of activity? In the business world they say "Every knock is a boost." It is! Because, if there is nothing good to say, the wise man says nothing! The conclusion is obvious that if a man does not praise, if he does not keep quiet—he is a "knocker" and has an axe of his own to grind at the expense of someone else. A person of real merit needs no advance agent; an article of real worth needs no advertising. Therefore, a

---

Art is not mere technical skill—it is the human echo of nature.—*Perry.*

person of true metal will come through calumny unscathed, and an article of honest value will "stand up" in spite of all the "knocking" it may receive. Explicitly: A certain make of instrument may be severely, often dishonorably, downed and discredited by a dealer. Perhaps this dealer is an agent for a rival firm of instrument manufacturers. In many cases these agents are retired or active players of instruments. The envy between some of them is astounding. They often resort to the worst kind of abuse regarding other makes in order to make a sale and obtain commission. Some stop at nothing, maliciously assailing other instruments and their makers, and often belittling and even blackmailing their players and advocates. And who suffers through this? The amateur—the beginner— the one who is not fully capable to judge an instrument. He is led on by the agent. Look out for the agent who "knocks" every other make of instrument but his own. Often those "knocked" are the best!

And so there is envy among performers. The envy that produces criticism of superiors, the envy that ridicules the efforts and accomplishments of others; which gives no credit for what has been accomplished and achieved. The envy which covets the accomplishment, the position, the standing of some-one else. The envy which, finding criticism so easy, condemns as crazy the man with a new idea or an original conception. And the extreme of egoism is the man whose envy puts in the absolute wrong any opinion which differs from his own.

There are teachers, too, who believe in the complete correctness of their own methods, and, believing, do not hesitate to discredit the methods of all other teachers. These are generally the teachers with more time than pupils on their hands. When a pupil does come to such a teacher, fault is immediately found with everything the pupil may have learned from a former instructor—or if the pupil has had no other teacher, abuse is heaped upon the names and reputations of other teachers. And is not such a teacher to be distrusted and avoided, as well as the dealer who "knocks"?

All people who have attained success are the prey of the people who are failures—or of those who have attempted to win success with but a pretense of effort. To these latter, the words "fakir" and "charlatan" come readily—quickly to be

---

Scales should never be "dry." If you are not interested in them, work with them until you become interested in them.—*Nicholas Rubinstein.*

applied (not where they belong, which would be too near "at home"), but to the very men whose success was achieved through merit, knowledge, and long experience. And because those of us who think, know that only through merit, knowledge and experience can success be won, we distrust the "knocker," dislike the envious man, and avoid him who has no good word for his fellows. All the "knocking" in the world could not take from a man one iota of his real merit, and the "knocker" only shows up his own narrow-mindedness, his envy, and his own lack of true worth.

Who seeks intelligently for facts as a foundation on which to ground any legitimate effort never fails.—*Plato*.

CHAPTER XXXIX.

THE REAL FAKIR AND THE REAL ARTIST

I. THE REAL FAKIR

In all criticism, it is generally the half-qualified layman, the person who knows a little of the subject in question—who is most eager to air his opinion, most harsh in his judgments and most regardless of the feelings of the person or persons criticized.

Many of these would-be critics are real fakirs. Fakirs in the sense of having little or no deep knowledge of any one thing, but a smattering of many things. Fakirs because they are opposed to new ideas, to new ways of doing things, which might show up their pretense to authority. What they cannot understand, they simply say is of no consequence, no value. According to these fakirs, anyone with a new idea, an advanced method, or a different way of doing things is called crazy, a crank, a fakir. It is a case of the "pot calling the kettle black."

In the musical world, there are many of these real fakirs. There are many who, in one branch or another, have had a little training, and feel that they "know it all." They cannot do anything as it really should be done, and therefore follow their own ideas and tastes. So, to save their own faces, they must call good musicians, and sincere artists, "fakirs." They knock their superiors, instead of learning from them; in short, they are jealous of the success of these good musicians. That must be the truth of it.

II. THE REAL ARTIST

Contrasted with the half studied, easily satisfied amateur or professional who sets himself up as critic of his superiors, we have those superiors themselves; the men who have seriously and painstakingly studied to reach the highest standard of their art. These are the real musicians, who in addition to hav-

---

Fingers are good servants but poor masters.—*Van Cleve.*

ing thoroughly mastered their own instruments, have a complete working knowledge of the theory of music. The true musician, be he teacher or player, is far less unkindly critical, and does not brand as a fakir anyone who does not believe as he does—whose ideas do not coincide exactly with his. No indeed! He often has to stand for much abuse from the real fakir, but it cannot hurt him, since the foundation upon which he stands is solid—being built upon intelligence, perseverence, hard work and experience.

As to criticism itself—no one can escape it. The most successful players and teachers, the greatest artists, are bound to come in for their share. It is an asset rather than an encumbrance. For was there ever a successful man who was not criticized? The person who receives only praise from his friends (so-called) is rarely a person of force or achievement. The greatest men in art, literature and history all had their critics. Even today Shakespeare has his detractors who claim that he did not write his own plays. Did the unkindly disposed men who surrounded Abraham Lincoln make him any less great? And did everyone agree with Theodore Roosevelt? Yet he was a great man who will live long in history. Do all of us admire and enjoy the music of Richard Wagner? No, but his works are very great just the same. This would be a dreary world if all of us had the same ideas and the same opinions. There would be little if any progress. Why, then, can we not be tolerant of the feelings and the beliefs of other people, even while we ourselves hold to our own ideas? Why can we not be generous enough to allow our neighbor the privilege of enjoying his own beliefs and of following his pursuits in his own way? In most cases, all derogatory remarks and all slanderous reports can be traced to their sources, and always rebound upon those who utter them.

And this applies to musicians in general and in particular. Many a teacher is called a "fakir" because he does not make a finished player of every pupil who comes to him. Another is called a "fakir" because the ignorant ones cannot appreciate his worth. And, many times, a fine artist or a surpassingly good teacher is slandered out of sheer malice. It is bad policy indeed for one teacher or performer to belittle another. Nine times out of ten, a musician who knocks another is jealous of his greater success—and equally often knows very little about the latter's methods and ability; yet it is he who presumes to judge. Yes, it is he who must be the "real fakir"—he who proves that "A little knowledge is a dangerous thing."

Charter Members of the American Bandmasters' Association (July 5th, 1929)

Seated—Left to Right.—A. Austin Harding, Arthur Pryor, Edwin Franko Goldman, Capt. Charles O'Neill

CHAPTER XL.

AMATEUR VS. PROFESSIONAL

In view of the fact that musical conditions have changed so extensively during the last years, few people seem to realize that one of the things that has hurt the professional musician and many professional organizations, is the amateur. There are amateur bands and orchestras in every city and town in the country. In large cities there are hundreds of such organizations. All of these organizations want some kind of an outlet for their activities, and they seek outlets of various kinds. An organization has to have occasions on which to play in public, after rehearsing for months. Every organization must play, or members will soon lose their interest and their enthusiasm.

In many instances and in many places, the services of these amateur organizations are sought, either because their services can be secured "gratis" or for less than the professional. Thus the amateur has crowded out the professional in many instances, and this is eminently unfair. Nobody has much sympathy for the unworthy professional, but how about those who are capable? Many musicians depend for their sustenance upon the very type of engagement that the amateur is taking away from him.

Amateurs *do not* or *should not* depend upon music for their livelihood. Professional musicians *do*. If professional musicians were to hinder amateurs at their real trades or professions, there would be much complaining. The amateur should really not expect to earn money through music, if he plays for love of the art as all amateurs should. That is, he should never accept money for any performance with the knowledge that he has taken an engagement from a professional. Amateur bands and orchestras should give concerts as frequently as possible for their friends and others who may be interested. They should raise money for the maintainance of their organizations through subscriptions or through their own concerts. They should play

---

Singleness, Simplicity and Clearness are the first essential elements of Instruction.
—*Comenius.*

for public charitable events occasionally. They should play as frequently as possible, but not attempt to take professional engagements. The motto "Live and let live" should be practiced.

All Amateur Bands and Orchestras have their rules and regulations. One of them should be never to accept money for an engagement for which professionals should be employed; another, never to accept an engagement that might keep professionals out of work. What a wonderful gesture this would be from the Amateur to the Professional! What new hope, interest and enthusiasm it would bring into his life! If this could be brought about, it would open up new fields to the professional, and would do much for the betterment of bands and band music. The number of amateur organizations is so overwhelming that the professional has but little chance, in most instances, to compete.

The amateur who follows music as an avocation should do everything possible to encourage the professional from whom he received his instruction and his inspiration. The professional should encourage the amateur. A better feeling and understanding should exist between these two types of musicians.

A great deal of animosity has been hurled at some of the service bands of the United States Army and Navy during the past few years. Professionals have felt that these bands were being paid by the government as Army and Navy musicians; and no one else in the service is permitted to engage in any outside business or enterprise. The law clearly states that service bands are not to compete with civilian bands under any condition or circumstances. It is clearly seen then, that the great danger to the professional is not the amateur, but the amateur who plays for money.

Amateur organizations can raise the dignity of their positions and gain the greater admiration and friendship of the professional as well as the layman by showing a desire to help the professional, and offering him the respect and consideration which he deserves. The entire cause of music will then be benefitted.

It might be well to explain that by "professional musician" I refer to that person who has been properly trained in music, and who devotes his time solely to music. By "amateur" I mean the player who takes up the study of music strictly as an avoca-

---

The way to fame is like the way to heaven—through much tribulation.—*Sterne*.

tion. There is another type of player called "semi-professional," who has some other business, trade or profession, and who uses music as a side line, to increase his income. "Semi-professional" players are as a rule not really good players. They cannot possibly be, because if their days are given over to other activities they cannot possibly give enough time to make and keep them proficient in the study of music or the study of the instrument. Many of the strictly amateur players are far superior to the so-called "semi-professionals." In this article I refer to the "semi-professional" as an amateur—and class him with the genuine amateur.

I am almost inclined to think that only men of genius understand each other fully and thoroughly.—*Schumann.*

CHAPTER XLI.

A GREAT FUTURE NEED

BANDS FOR HIGH SCHOOL GRADUATES

America has every reason to be proud of what she is accomplishing through the School Bands. These bands should be given every possible moral and financial encouragement, for they wield a great influence for good over those who come under their guidance. But what becomes of these thousand of players after they leave school? In many instances, the instruments are the property of the organizations or the schools. When the students are graduated many of them are, therefore, left without an instrument. They secure positions and enter upon a business career and it may be several years before they can save enough money to purchase an instrument. By that time they have lost their playing ability and realize that it will take considerable practice and study to regain all that they have lost, and as a consequence most of them become discouraged and never again make an attempt to play. This is a great pity, indeed, for nothing can excel the joy that is derived from music as an avocation. It helps to occupy many a long hour, and brings comfort, relaxation and uplift.

It is my hope that in the near future some way will be found whereby the students who are now a part of these High School and other bands may be kept interested after they are graduated from school. Alumni or adult bands will in all probability be formed in all communities, for it seems a great pity that so many of these school players should never perform again after they leave school. I know the need and actual desire for these amateur adult bands, and I prophesy that the day is not far off when the school player will be able to continue his interest in band-playing in some sort of "post-graduate" band.

Just how these adult bands can be brought about is difficult to say, but they are bound to come. All of the youngsters who

---

Music is God's best gift to man, the only art of heaven given to earth, the only art of earth we take to heaven.—*Landon.*

learned to play an instrument in their school days, will appreciate the value of their instruction more as they grow older. As they mature they will begin to realize what an important factor music is in one's life. The instruments are taken away from them when they would just begin to secure the greatest benefits from them. Every city should have an adult band, where all those interested in music may go once or twice a week to play. Perhaps the schools will foster this movement. They can do much for the promotion of such a plan, by offering the use of their buildings for rehearsals. Just how to provide the graduates with instruments is a great problem, but it must and will be solved soon. The amateur musician must be encouraged. We want and need more music lovers, and more music enthusiasts. When it is made possible for all these youthful students to continue their musical activities after they leave school, we will have made a great step toward being a more musical nation. It is going to be a great help to our professional musicians too. All in all, it will be an advancement of the cause of music in general.

Many students, who own their instruments, lose interest in their playing after leaving High School when they find that there is no amateur adult band in their community which they may join. This idea of the adult amateur band is one to which those who are interested in the band movement in America should give serious thought and attention. The graduate should not be permitted to drop his instrument or lose his interest in music. He should immediately be able to transfer his musical activities to another organization which offers him cultural and social advantages, besides the purely musical ones.

To me, it is with Bach as if the eternal harmonies discoursed with one another.
—*Goethe.*

CHAPTER XLII.

THE BAND FROM AN EDUCATIONAL, ARTISTIC AND CULTURAL VIEWPOINT

OPINIONS OF FAMOUS ORCHESTRAL CONDUCTORS, COMPOSERS, AND OTHER FAMOUS MEN.

Great music is a human necessity and a public service. Bands in procession and public gardens give joy to everyone from the children to the most experienced musician.

DR. LEOPOLD STOKOWSKI
Conductor of the Philadelphia Symphony Orchestra.

Good bands are altogether too rare. For too many of us a band means simply a miscellaneous group of brass instruments, rather monotonous perhaps in tone color. But a great band with the woodwinds as well as the brass, can produce music of a peculiar magnificence. I admire what Mr. Goldman has done to spread the appreciation of good band music. When I see the deserted band stands in our city parks—or the place where there once were band stands—I wish for a happier day when this truly popular form of music may be restored to us in all the open places where we seek recreation and inspiration.

DR. JOHN ERSKINE
Author, Pianist, and President of the Juilliard School of Music.

I am glad of this opportunity of expressing my conviction that the modern band is an absolutely indispensable medium of musical expression.

I feel this because it is obvious that any medium occupying a position so close to the hearts of the people as the Band must always be encouraged and expanded in order that we all may get the full benefits of its cultural value.

JOHN ALDEN CARPENTER
Noted American Composer.

Art is with us that we shall not perish of too much truth.—*Nietzsche.*

176

I consider the band of the utmost importance in the development of music in this country, especially among the young people familiarizing them as it does with the masterpieces of musical literature. With a few notable exceptions the artistic possibilities of the band have not been developed in this country as they have been in Europe. In this age of progress, especially in the public schools, the band is coming to the fore, and assuming the importance which it really deserves.

DR. HENRY HADLEY
Famous American Composer and Conductor.

Please allow me to express to Edwin Franko Goldman my cordial respect for the work he is doing through the development of bands and band music. Thousands of our young people are learning to know and love good music through playing in bands. The view sometimes expressed that the band is a sort of poor relation in the musical family seems to me snobbish and misleading. The band is not inferior to the orchestra or the string quartet, but different, having its own place, qualities and service. It sometimes seems to me that it serves music something as the story of adventure serves literature. We do not expect the subtlety of Henry James or Meredith in a story by Dumas or Stevenson. Yet in their own place the latter are as fine as any literature can be. So with the band; if it lacks the range and reach of the orchestra, the subtlety and intimateness of the quartet, it has its own delightful vigor, precision, color, and verve,—delightful to all sincere and spontaneous music-lovers. And while no doubt the greatest things in music literature are for orchestra and chamber music groups, there is plenty of fine band music too. The true success of a band as of an orchestra depends on playing only the best in music—among which I put the stirring vigor of a Sousa march and the grace of a Strauss waltz as well as Bach or Beethoven, Tschaikowsky or Wagner.

DR. DANIEL GREGORY MASON
MacDowell Professor of Music—Columbia University, N. Y.

A well conducted band is an excellent educational agency. The absolute precision needed for the playing of the right tones in the right manner in harmony with the efforts of the entire group makes for alertness and cooperation. The thrill of the

There is not a fiercer hell than failure in a great object.—*Keats.*

music makes for well-being and kindliness. Pride in the accomplishment of the organization and the contribution it makes to civic life help to build better citizens. Mr. Goldman has my warm endorsement in band betterment, because making better boys and girls means a better America.

PROF. PETER W. DYKEMA
Professor of Music Education—Teachers College,
Columbia University, N. Y.

It seems to me that there is no sort of musical organization more capable of an influence for good from a cultural standpoint than the Band, for under normal circumstances, it is within easier reach of those who most need this influence.

But apart from this matter of the civic or social importance of bands, what interests me most about the band is the tremendous possibility for artistic expression through this medium. The Band is altogether different from the orchestra, and has its own idiom, though composers have been very slow in realizing it. The sooner we get away from thinking of the Band as the step-sister of the Orchestra, and from performing music on the Band which was written for, and sounds better on, the Orchestra, the sooner will we have taken the most necessary step ahead.

Bandmen, and even band directors, have been largely at fault in this for the simple reason that they have not realized the importance of being highly trained musicians, as distinct from being merely highly trained performers. Many of them are in a rut, artistically speaking, and are not forward-looking men. The musical appreciation of many of them is but rudimentary.

When band musicians are on a par in every respect with the finest orchestral musicians, and when the Band has a literature of its own, not composed merely of arrangements, marches, medleys—castoffs, but of great symphonic works, then will we feel that we have reached our goal and accomplished our destiny. More than any other one person in America, Mr. Edwin Franko Goldman has shown the way, and by the example of his own band has demonstrated what can be done, granted the possession of the necessary fundamental musicianship and the will to achieve.

LEO SOWERBY
Famous American Composer.

Love teacheth music.—*Plato.*

Ever since man has made music, there has been the human tendency to play together in groups of instruments. Probably the first bands consisted of drums, cistrums and a few wind instruments. Gradually through the centuries there evolved the modern band, which even at this day is still subject to change, but the influence of the band in both war and peace, has been so extraordinary and so obvious that it seems more or less useless to comment upon it.

From a musical and artistic standpoint the modern band is a very flexible means of expression, which can accommodate itself to all kinds of music, from the popular song to the great symphonic and orchestra works. The fact that bands are cropping up everywhere in the United States is partly attributed to the training received in public schools and partly to the prestige of such famous bands as the Sousa Band and the Goldman Band. These organizations are distinctly valuable to the state, in that they provide a source of inspiration as well as entertainment. Millions of people in our country find them a relief from the strenuous obligations of life. Every good band is a decided asset to the community of which it is a part. Mr. Edwin Franko Goldman's fine spirit of idealism and his wholesome unselfishness, together with his rare training in both the symphonic and the band field, have been of very great importance to this movement.

DR. JAMES FRANCIS COOKE
President—Presser Foundation.

I am deeply interested to hear that Edwin Franko Goldman, that master of bandmasters, has written a book on "Band Betterment." May it come into the hands of many band leaders, and may it inspire young people to form bands. A book like this should be of great assistance to all people interested in this type of music.

It has always been my sincere belief that playing a musical instrument not only is a matter of individual joy and pleasure, but also is a great help in developing a deeper appreciation and understanding of music.

It is most gratifying to note the improvement in the artistic value of band programs in recent years, and I know

---

The root of all brilliant playing lies in one thing—accuracy. Without accuracy any attempt at brilliancy must result in mussiness.—*Teresa Carreno.*

that Mr. Goldman's book will be an inspiration towards this goal: higher class music for everyone.

WILLEM VAN HOOGSTRATEN
*Conductor of the Portland Symphony Orchestra, and
N. Y. Stadium Summer Concerts.*

There can be no possible doubt in the mind of anyone who has at heart the welfare of music that the band is a potent influence in the promotion of the finest art. At an age in which the taste of young people is being formed, the band in high-schools and colleges accomplishes much in directing it in effective channels. It gives, too, a practical interest in music to students who take part in the rehearsals and performances. Band music has done much, I believe, to carry good music to multitudes of people who have not had the opportunity to listen to orchestras; and even where orchestras are available, there are numberless music-lovers who have taken joy in band performances such as those admirable concerts that the Goldman Band has given in the summer in New York. There was a day, to be sure, in which the quality of band programs left something—sometimes much—to be desired; but that day has been followed by a finer dawn. It is a matter for regret, however, that composers are not more directly interested in the creation of band music and that so much of the band repertory of first-class compositions has to be made up of arrangements. Wagner set a good example when he wrote his March of Homage for military band, but few of his successors have followed it.

FELIX BOROWSKI
Composer, Pianist, Author and Critic. Chicago, Ill.

The announcement that Mr. Goldman is about to publish a book on Bands and Band music is something to look forward to with a great deal of anticipation by thousands of lovers of that branch of music, and to me, with my great interest in this particular subject, one of much pleasure.

The advance in the last ten years has truly been marvelous in every respect, be it in the matter of instrumentation, conducting, or type of music. It is also most significant that composers from Italy, France, England and Canada, as well as

---

The eye of the master will do more work than both his hands.—*Franklin.*

from our own country now have turned to this field for musical expression. With his many years of active service, such as the annual series of concerts in New York with his magnificent organization, and his participation as Judge and Conductor at Contests and Festivals throughout the States, Mr. Goldman brings to this subject all the qualifications necessary.

Dr. Carl Busch
Composer, Conductor, and Honorary Member of the American Bandmasters' Association.

My interest in the military band as a means of musical expression dates from the time I conducted the 301st Infantry Regimental Band of eighty-five members during the World War, and at the same time directed the A. E. F. School for Bandmasters founded by Dr. Walter Damrosch at the request of General Pershing, at Chaumont, France. Although the military bands at that time were used largely to uphold the morale of our troops and the general populace during war-time, it was always quite evident to me that this form of instrumental combination was capable of disseminating a definite love and understanding of the best in music. Because of the greater ease with which most of the wind instruments can be learned as opposed to the mastery of a stringed instrument, the band seems to me to be a practical form of community organization. Having in mind the splendid arrangements and original compositions that have been written for the wind band I feel quite confident in its future development.

Albert Stoessel
Conductor, Composer and Violinist.

If our country as a whole is to become truly cultured, musically, greater stress must be laid on developing local talent, as opposed to dependence on occasional concerts by symphonic orchestras or other musical organizations of national fame. Every community should support the highest type of orchestra or brass band for which talent is available or can be developed, and the artistic excellence attained by such organizations as The Goldman Band, which has been well named a "Symphony in Brass," admits of no doubt that the brass band should rank high as an instrument of culture.

The most certain sign of wisdom is a continual cheerfulness.—*Montaigne.*

Great strides have already been made in this direction, despite the fact that the broadcasting by radio of symphony concerts and grand opera from coast to coast presents an added temptation to lie back and absorb enjoyment and culture by turning a button. If the radio is not to prove a positive detriment to our musical growth, this temptation should be recognized and overcome by a realization that a community becomes musical in the best sense more through the music which it makes for itself than through the music which is made for it. The radio can be of service by supplying a stimulating standard of interpretation, but by all means let the multiplication and betterment of bands continue throughout the land until our nation shall become second to none in the practice and appreciation of music.

ERNEST T. CARTER
American Composer and formerly Lecturer on Music at Princeton University.

A man who has reached a certain kind of preeminence in his art, as Mr. Goldman has done, as a musical conductor, merits the interest and attention of all who believe in the culture of people. Music is a great factor in that respect; for the appreciation of good music, like the appreciation of drama, helps to put forward the best elements in human nature. The more one hears good music, the more appreciative becomes the mind to fine things in life.

Music, as an art, is a great help also to the stage; for the actor who understands music becomes a better actor for understanding that art. It gives him, not only a sense of spiritual beauty, but it stimulates his sense of rhythm and effect, as a dramatic actor.

Mr. Goldman has done more to stimulate and interest the popular mind in the works of the best composers, than many I know. His selections have been in good taste, and made with good judgment; and he has thus created a desire for all who are interested in listening to the great works of the great composers.

DANIEL FROHMAN
Famous Theatrical Manager and Producer.

The profane never hear music; the holy ever hear it. It is God's voice, the divine breath audible.—*Thoreau.*

The importance of school bands and orchestras in our musical life is very great. They are laying a foundation of music experience among our young people which has already shown itself to be of great value for our musical development.

I am very glad to have an opportunity to express my deep appreciation for the splendid work Mr. Goldman has done toward the cultivation of higher standards of music in this country, especially in the field of band music. He has always maintained high standards of taste and performance, and the experience and knowledge of this branch of music which he has attained and which will be perpetuated and made available for others through the medium of his book on the subject of band leadership, will do much for the cultivation of the art of music in America.

FREDERICK S. CONVERSE
Distinguished American Composer.

The value of music as a normal part of education is now commonly recognized, and in schools of all grades American boys and girls are receiving helpful training in some form of music.

I wish to commend the efforts that are being made to organize and train school bands, which afford a good opportunity for musical expression.

A boy has a wide range of choice of instruments and that is important. He can find something to his liking and devote himself to that.

His school contacts become stronger through his music than through any other subject in the curriculum.

Best of all, his knowledge of musical literature develops interestingly.

Thanks to some of our enlightened bandmasters, like Edwin Franko Goldman, the best things in music have been arranged for band playing, and as the school band progresses, each member of it intensifies an appreciation of musical masterpieces.

Band competitions have been organized all over the country. It is a good movement, and has educational merit of high value.

I hope bands will increase and flourish in this country. That is one very good way to make America musical.

DR. EUGENE A. NOBLE
Secretary—The Juilliard Foundation.

I hold no truer truth obtainable by man than comes of music.—*Browning.*

I am delighted to learn that out of the wealth of his experience Mr. Goldman is to contribute a book on the improvement of bands. Such a work is urgently needed, and will be of inestimable assistance.

Surely, no one who has heard his organization and a few others in America, can doubt the importance of a Band, or question its beauty, its power, or its flexibility. There was a time when the word "band" evoked but little enthusiasm in the minds of musicians; but, thanks to a few men, such as he, this is no longer the case. Today, one is forced to recognize its value as a medium of artistic expression, and to accept it as a most important aid to cultural advancement.

Given the advantage of a conductor who possesses adequate technical knowledge, the Band is a superb instrument. Too often failure may be attributed solely to the conductor's ignorance. I am sure this book will prevent just this sort of thing.

BAINBRIDGE CRIST
Well-known American Composer.

It has long been my conviction that bands are of the greatest importance in the development of musical life in America.

To take an example: For the budding composer, the strings offer no problem, as nearly everywhere he can easily become acquainted with their technical propensities. For the wind instruments, however, this is a different proposition entirely, and as each of them calls for special treatment, it is naturally of the greatest importance that he should have opportunities of becoming acquainted with them. But more than that, the band can be, and should be made to be, an artistic entity in itself.

Any one who has ever heard any of the really great bands knows the practically limitless artistic possibilities of a really first-class organization of that character. Besides which, there is a literature which fits only a band and not a symphony orchestra, although there are many symphonic works which can be played with equal or nearly equal effect by a band.

I have not mentioned the stirring quality of the great marches and other typically out-of-door compositions, but, from the foregoing, I think that you will realize that any action

---

Music itself is in a measure the expression of its time.—*Philip Hale.*

which will improve the condition of those bands already exist-
ing, and create new ones everywhere will have my whole-
hearted endorsement.

HANS KINDLER
Conductor of the National Symphony Orchestra,
Washington, D.C.

It is undoubtedly true that largely owing to the influence
of the radio the interest in music has been multiplied manifold
throughout our country. This is as it should be, as the great
population of a country so vast as ours should not depend on the
few larger cities scattered throughout the country for its musical
nourishment. Every town and village should have its own
musical organization in which the individual players, well
grounded in the technique of their instruments, can properly
take their part. I welcome every effort made by our better
leading musicians to raise the standard of such organizations
and to encourage them in the cultivation of music in its highest
form.

DR. WALTER DAMROSCH
Famous Symphony Conductor.

I was interested, indeed, to read that Edwin Franko Goldman has written a book entitled "Band Betterment". I think
that such a book is filling a decided want and doubt if anybody
could be more qualified to write such a book than a man of
his extraordinary experience.

While nothing is further from my mind than to say that
the string orchestras in this country are ideal, there is no
question but that thousands of bands, professional and otherwise, are in dire need of assistance, such as I am sure this book
will give them.

Bands in general, already suffer in comparison to symphony
orchestras, insofar as the symphony orchestras have the advantage of having the literature of the great masters at their
disposal, while bands have mostly to play scores which have
been reorchestrated for that purpose.

There is no reason why a good band should not give the
same service for the music enjoyment of an interested public
in open air as a symphony orchestra gives in a closed hall. In

---

Music touches every key of memory.—*L. E. Landon.*

the end, it will all depend on the man who is at the head of the band, and I am sure that most of these band leaders will be only too eager to profit by the book Mr. Goldman has written. I am confident, therefore, that this book will meet with the great success it deserves.　ALFRED HERTZ

Former Conductor of the Metropolitan Opera Company, N. Y.
Conductor of the San Francisco Symphony Orchestra.

I have read with much interest of the book Mr. Goldman has just written and which is no doubt bound to make its way throughout the entire country. He is the very one to write such a book because his name and his extraordinary ability as a band conductor par excellence are known to every person in the country that ever heard any music.

The depression has played havoc with all branches of music and it is to be hoped that the great renaissance of our art is not far off. This rebirth of musical activities will no doubt include bands, professional ones as well as others. My hearty wishes go out to Mr. Goldman that he may see this new life in its full bloom and that every city in America, large and small, will once more have band music as we used to have it in the good old times. There is an important place for a band in every community and its activities can have a very fine artistic and cultural influence. A united effort on the part of the American Bandmasters' Association in regard to program propositions will be a great help to those band leaders who are far from the large cities. I have conducted a band only once in my life and I remember the experience with great pleasure.

RUDOLPH GANZ
Distinguished Pianist and Conductor.

The book "Band Betterment" will, no doubt, be a most interesting and helpful document. The importance of good bands in the life of any community cannot be valued highly enough, as music is a splendid means of spiritual and educational development. It is remarkable how many good bands we have in the United States today, and it shows that the desire for good music is getting stronger from year to year. A well trained band will help to create a music-loving and understanding audience.　ARTUR BODANZKY

Conductor—Metropolitan Opera Company, N. Y.

Music, when soft voices die, vibrates in the memory.—*Shelley.*

The band and its development in the future rests upon the effort composers, conductors, and musicians will extend in this direction.

We all recognize the importance and the possibilities of the band. School and professional bands must extend their libraries, and make it as interesting and individualistic as possible.

In a symphony orchestra, arrangements are nearly always traditional, and done by the composer. In band literature each leader can go far in making his band stand out by special arrangements. He is not bound down by tradition. What a marvelous field it leaves open for an energetic bandmaster!

Furthermore, the band leader can use almost any new combination of instruments he desires—the many strange effects and tonal colors are endless.

Bands have had their place in the artistic world for many years, and as far as I can see ahead, they are going to march along as long as their Standard Bearers have the courage to blaze the path with sincere effort, and artistic ideals.

NATHANIEL SHILKRET
Conductor—Victor Talking Machine Co.
Famous Broadcasting Conductor and Composer.

I welcome the opportunity to add my voice to those of the many thousands of people in this country who enthusiastically approve of the concert band movement now in such splendid process of development.

For many years during my numerous concert tours throughout the States I have urged wherever possible the creation and encouragement of school bands in the interest of culture and happiness. It is gratifying to note the extent to which musical performance is today recognized by enlightened public opinion, supported by educational authority as a most important element in the life of a civilized community.

That the school bands require professionally trained organizations performing in public as an incentive goes of course without saying, and for this reason, if for no other, every effort should be made to bring public bands to the highest possible point of artistic efficiency. Apart from that, however, a fine public band playing in suitable surroundings is of absolutely incalculable value in its power to bring to the people the under-

---

Music is love; it springs from religion and leads to religion.—*Hanslick.*

standing and the enjoyment of leisure and it is to be hoped that the civic pride so characteristic of many American cities will create a determination to achieve the utmost everywhere.

The magnificent results Mr. Goldman has accomplished with the Goldman Band and his lifelong experience in the particular field of band music give exceptional weight to his counsels and I feel sure that his book on "Band Betterment" will be eagerly received. I look forward to the time to come when the public performances of a concert band built up in accordance with the artistic standards he has established will be a distinguishing feature of every town, great and small, in our country.

HAROLD BAUER
World-renowned Pianist
and President of Beethoven Association

One of the outstanding phases of musical development in our country has to do with the significant growth in the quality of the concert band. The band has always been the most democratic of professional ensembles, and has probably had more direct influence on the musical life of the nation than any other form of musical expression. Where the symphonic orchestra has influenced thousands, the bands have had their tens of thousands. This influence is extended from the small town to the metropolis, and has permeated music education from the secondary schools to the universities.

Unfortunately in the past the two matters of the extent of influence and the quality of influence have not balanced one another. For a good many years the quality of the band repertory was, as a general rule, of mediocre standard. With the passing of years, due to the outstanding work of such men as Edwin Franko Goldman, Austin Harding of the University of Illinois, James Gillette, of Carleton College, and many others, the concert band has assumed a new place in musical life. The repertory has been greatly increased through judicious arrangements of works from the symphonic repertory, and has been further expanded by original works written for the concert band. At the same time the band itself has been the subject of much serious study, and its instrumentation has evolved from the military brass band with its limited range of expression to the

---

There is always room for a man of force, and he makes room for many.—*Emerson.*

fully equipped symphonic band capable of as many variations of symphonic coloring in its field as is the symphony orchestra.

It is to be hoped that the American composers will take both the opportunity and the responsibility which comes to them in this manner, and add significant works to the band repertory. The possibilities for the composer in this field are wide, and he has, furthermore, the opportunity of speaking his message to tremendous audiences through the medium of the thousands of excellent bands all over the country. This is a development which promises well for the future.

HOWARD HANSON
American Composer, Director Eastman School of Music,
Rochester, N. Y.

If there still is any doubt about the usefulness and artistic efficacy of competent brass bands, I do not know in which circle it exists.

Time was, when owing to the few varieties of brass instruments, their structural defects, and limited range, a band was looked upon purely as a medium for the performance of military and popular (also light) compositions.

All that is changed now, for we have perfect brass instruments of many kinds that approximate those of a symphony orchestra, we have better players, with the modern technic required; we have excellent musicians to write specifically for band or adapt symphony repertoire; and we have highly gifted conductors who are not only drillmasters but also interpreters. I am glad to place Mr. Goldman eminently in that list for I know what thorough musical training he received before he exchanged his solo instrument for the baton.

I have heard Beethoven, Wagner, and other classical masters performed by bands and must admit that when the interpretations were authentic, they gave me real artistic pleasure.

Of course, the greatest value of a band is that it appeals directly to the masses of the people, and that its instruments induce desire in the young, to play them. In that way, by using much good music, a band instills a higher taste not only in the performers, but also in the rank and file of listeners.

I wish America more, better and bigger bands, to emulate the Goldman example.

LEONARD LIEBLING
Editor—The Musical Courier.

He who has not been a servant cannot become a praisworthy master.—*Plato.*

The amazing number of School Bands in all sections of the United States, said to be more than 100,000, complicates an already serious problem—the lack of competent leadership. The rapid multiplication of bands has outstripped the supply of capable leaders. It is not the fault of the boys and girls in the bands that far too large a proportion of the organizations make more noise than music, that the players do not develop a refined musical taste, that their tone is raucous and unmusical.

No man in the United States can do more to solve this problem than Mr. Goldman. His own incomparable band is a constant object lesson; his wide and intimate contact with school bands in every section of the United States has endeared him to thousands of boys and girls and their leaders; he has the full confidence of the entire country; his prestige, personal and professional, is unique. His enormous influence will be exerted in building the Symphonic Band, with its refinement of tone and musicianly interpretation of worthy music.

So all bands, band leaders and lovers of band music will welcome Mr. Goldman's book, "Band Betterment". May its success parallel that of its author.

Dr. Hollis Dann
Director, Department of Music Education,
New York University.

At Easter time at the old Moravian Church of Winston-Salem, N.C., the venerable Bishop stands on the steps in the early morn and says, "Christ is Risen, Christ Is Risen Indeed!" He is immediately answered by a great band of four hundred instruments divided into separate units, answering antiphonally. The effect of this band is one of the most thrilling parts of this service. One of the greatest effects of this wonderful service, however, is the part it has played in the lives of the young people. Every child hopes some day to play in this band and it has, as a result, made this town a musical community.

The band has possibilities which we have not fully realized, as shown by the above illustration. It can uplift and inspire a community in its educational as well as in its religious life. The goal for which we are all working is not more professional musicians but more music that is made by the people themselves. I congratulate Edwin Franko Goldman upon the part he has had in helping people to make their own music.

John Finley Williamson, *Pres.,*
Westminster Choir School, Princeton, N. J.

In Europa ist überall dort die Musik zu einer Volksleiden-
schaft geworden, wo die Kirche, dem Beispiel orientalischer
Kulte folgend, das Volk zur Musik herangezogen hat. Weniger
tief wirkt die blosse Befriedigung des Amüsierbedürfnisses, wie
die Länder zeigen, wo der Tanz sich an die Masse wendet:
Hort denn der Tänzer was ihn bewegt?

Musik sucht nicht Berauschte, sondern Begeisterte und
darum bietet sich Ihrer Bandenbewegung eine so grosse Aus-
sicht. Denn für ein Amüsement werden Sie vielleicht mehrere
hundert tausend Banden *aufstellen*. Aber wenn Sie einhundert-
tausend Banden *zusammenhalten* können, so kann nur Be-
geisterung das Band sein.

ARNOLD SCHOENBERG
World-famous Composer.

Too many people have wrong ideas about a Band; several
of the great composers have written original works for Bands,
and some of them today in Europe play transcriptions not only
of the great classics but of the best moderns also, and being
heard by the most sophisticated audiences have been received
with respect and admiration.

In the hands of true musicians with a real knowledge of
their art, bands can do much to develop the love of great music.

VLADIMIR GOLSCHMANN
Conductor of The St. Louis Symphony Orchestra.

The important place that fine bands have held in my own
and the other countries of Europe is well known to the Americans
who have lived abroad. It has had great musical value in
Europe and I feel that the opportunity for the American public
to enjoy the band music will be greater and greater as the
results of public school music education become more and more
evident. The excellent arrangements of classical music which
have distinguished the Goldman Band programs set the right
example.

I am glad to know that Mr. Goldman has written a book
which can serve as guide and help to concert bands and bandmasters.

ARTHUR RODZINSKI
Conductor of The Cleveland Orchestra.

The beginning is half of the whole, and we all praise a good beginning.—*Plato.*

I am in hearty sympathy with the purpose of Mr. Goldman's book "Band Betterment" and endorse the effort to promote the interest for bands and band-music in America.

Band-music reaches the people in a direct way and has its immediate effect: the first interest and attention for music is roused. I therefore believe that the improvement of bands and band music could be most beneficial for the musical education of this vast country.

SERGE KOUSSEVITZKY
Conductor of the Boston Symphony Orchestra.

Probably the most intense aesthetic experiences of early childhood were those thrills awakened by the tones of a brass band. As an evidence of the powerful influence of this class of music, one need but recall those groups of children that inevitably follow the bands that accompanied the migratory circus or theatrical company.

Doubtless in many cases, these experiences were the beginnings of a fondness for music of a polyphonic character, and created a taste for a variety of tone color that the beginner does not at first derive from the piano or reed-organ.

Then too, when we consider how remarkable has been the development of brass instruments in respect to facility of execution, delicacy of expression and tone quality, it is not strange that our band-conductors should take delight in presenting programs ever increasing in artistic value. In listening to the finely rendered selections from the *Nibelungen Trilogy*, *Tristan and Isolde*, and movements from the best of standard works, one is convinced that our park bands are exerting a great influence in behalf of high grade music and that they constitute an educational factor of unquestionable value.

EDGAR STILLMAN KELLEY
Noted American Composer.

Imitation is natural to man from his infancy. Man differs from other animals particularly in this, that he is imitative, and acquires his rudiments of knowledge in this way; besides, the delight in it is universal.—*Aristotle.*

The history of music in the United States during the past half-century is one of continuous and in many ways extra-ordinary progress toward a high artistic goal in practically every field of the art save one: the wind-band. Orchestras, choral societies, chamber-music groups, operatic organizations of the first rank—all have achieved an artistic standard of high degree.

But this standard could not have been attained had not these various organizations been faithful to the principles which experience has proved indispensable to success. Among these are efficient leadership, and capable and well-disciplined mem-bership, ensuring adequate and intelligent rehearsal; the culti-vation of a distinctive and sound repertoire; attention to the important art of program-making; and finally, effective publicity and the grasp of opportunity for public service.

Among those musicians who have been conspicuous in their fidelity to just such principles, none is better fitted to lead a forward movement than Mr. Edwin Franko Goldman. His work in New York and elsewhere for the cause of better band music is too well known to require more than grateful acknowl-edgement, and gives all the more reason to welcome the ap-pearance of such a book as the one he is about to publish.

The raising of our band music—in all but a few instances—to anything approaching the familiar standards of our best orchestras demands the establishment of a reasonably uniform and scientifically ordered instrumentation; the development of a band literature based thereon, and giving encouragement to composition, rather than arrangement, for band; and con-scientious, regular, efficiently conducted rehearsal. No one of these three elements may be neglected.

The tremendous impetus of the High School Band move-ment must not be overlooked. Properly and conservatively directed, it should prove a power for good in the further develop-ment of our musical system. Not bigger, but better bands should be the ideal; and in all these matters Mr. Goldman's leadership will be of untold value.

WALLACE GOODRICH
Director, New England Conservatory of Music, Boston, Mass.

It is by pictures and music, by art and song and symbolic representations, that all nations have been educated in their adolescence.—*Kingsley*.

‛AMOUS GOLDMAN MARCHES FOR BAND

. B. A. (American Bandmasters Association)
OY SCOUTS OF AMERICA
ANADIAN NATIONAL EXHIBITION
ENTRAL PARK
HEROKEE
OLUMBIA (6-8)
AGLE EYES
MBLEM OF FREEDOM
ET FREEDOM RING
IARCH ELECTRIC
IISCHA ELMAN
N THE AIR
N THE ALERT
N THE CAMPUS
N THE FARM
N THE GO

*ON THE HUNT
*ON THE MALL
*ON THE PIER (6-8)
*ON THE ROAD
ON PARADE
*ONWARD-UPWARD
THE PIONEER
*PRIDE OF AMERICA
RADIO CITY
*SAGAMORE
*SPIRIT OF PEACE
*SPIRIT OF YOUTH
*STEPPING ALONG
*SUNAPEE (6-8)
*THE THIRD ALARM
UNIVERSITY (Grand March)
*YOUNG AMERICA (6-8)

ese marches are also published for orchestra.

e: The above marches (with the exception of *Emblem of Freedom, Let Freedom Ring, Mischa Elman* and *University*) are also published for Piano Solo.

MISCELLANEOUS COMPOSITIONS
For Band or Orchestra

BIT OF SYNCOPATION. One Step.

THE TWILIGHT. Fox Trot (Orch. only)

N THE GREEN. Valse Intermezzo.

*STAR OF THE EVENING. Valse.

*SPRINGTIME FANCIES. Valse Intermezzo (Orch. only)
*SUNSHINE AND SHADOWS. Waltz (Band only)

so Published for Piano Solo.

THE GOLDMAN BAND LIBRARY

Musical Works in the Repertory of the Goldman Band, edited under the supervision of Edwin ranko Goldman. Clear indications for correct interpretation are given in detail, in accordance ith the actual renditions of the Goldman Band. Standard and Concert Instrumentation.

.A. March. Goldman
ANTINO—Lemare
RKIES' JUBILEE—Turner
TRANCE and MARCH of PEERS
om "Iolanthe"—Sullivan-Lake
NTING SCENE (A)—Bucalossi
LY COPPERSMITH (The)—Characteristic Novelty March—Peters
L NIDRE. Hebrew Melody. Transc. based
a version of Max Bruch

LA GOLONDRINA. Mexican Waltz-Serenade
MARCH ELECTRIC—Goldman.
ON THE ROAD—Goldman
ONWARD and UPWARD. March—Goldman
SLEEPERS, WAKE. J. S. Bach—Al Chiaffarelli
STEPPING ALONG. March—Goldman
THIRD ALARM. (The). March—Goldman
WALTZ IN A MAJOR—Joh. Brahms
YOUNG AMERICA. March—Goldman